AUTHORS
TAKE
SIDES
ON IRAQ
AND THE GULF WAR

AUTHORS TAKE SIDES ON IRAQ AND THE GULF WAR

Edited by

JEAN MOORCROFT WILSON and CECIL WOOLF

CECIL WOOLF PUBLISHERS, LONDON

First published in 2004
by Cecil Woolf Publishers, 1 Mornington Place, London NW1 7RP
Tel: 020 7387 2394

British Library Cataloguing-in-Publication Data
A catalogue record of this book is available from the British Library

ISBN 1-897967-43-8

Printed and bound by TJ International Ltd, Padstow, Cornwall

Contents

Introduction

This book is about two wars, separated by twelve years but united by the figures of Saddam Hussein and George Bush father and son. It is, in part, an attempt to record contemporary opinions and reactions to two of the most contentious issues of our times, the Gulf War of 1991 and the Iraq invasion of 2003. The fourth in a series of 'Authors Take Sides', its intention, like its predecessors, is to be both informative and thought-provoking.

It was in June 1937 that Nancy Cunard circulated a questionnaire, signed by W.H. Auden, Louis Aragon and Stephen Spender, to 150 writers, asking:

Are you for, or against, the legal Government and the people of Republican Spain?

Are you for, or against, Franco and Fascism?

The answers were published in *Authors Take Sides on the Spanish War*. Using that booklet as their inspiration in 1967, Cecil Woolf and John Bagguley canvassed the views of writers on the Vietnam War and in 1982 Cecil Woolf and Jean Moorcroft Wilson collected the opinions of writers on the Falklands conflict. The significant difference between Nancy Cunard's *Authors Take Sides on the Spanish War* and its successors, however, is that whereas the purpose of the original booklet was, primarily, to arouse the indignation of its contributors, the present collection of writings, like those on Vietnam and the Falklands, is intended to present a truthful picture: to stimulate debate. While we had our own personal views on the issues – in fact, started out on different sides in both conflicts – our aim in canvassing the opinions of authors was, so far as possible, to present an objective record of a cross-section of the intellectual community.

To that end we approached writers in the broadest sense – novelists, poets, playwrights, journalists, as well as authors in specialized fields, such as history, philosophy, science and politics. Only in a few cases where writers were also politicians did we consciously balance our selection by inviting those of different persuasions to contribute. Otherwise authors were chosen regardless of any known opinions, since we wanted to obtain a random mix. No pressure was put on anyone to reply and no effort was made to influence the outcome. All replies attempting to answer the questions, or discussing the issues involved, have been included. And apart from the occasional grammatical correction to pieces by foreign contributors, or unless specifically requested by authors, there has been no editing. In this we have been guided by the Spanish writer, Salvador de Madriaga's advice, that 'men of letters should have the freedom to bring you their flowers with stems, roots and even some earth attached to them'.

Whereas for the Vietnam book authors from 35 countries were invited to participate, for the Gulf and Iraq conflicts we concentrated on the British and Americans, together with a sprinkling of Arab and European writers. One of the most significant facts to emerge from the Iraq questionnaire was the extraordinarily low response rate from American authors, even allowing for the difficulties of working through literary agents and publishers and the vagaries of transatlantic post. Out of over forty approached, fewer than half a dozen replied. Readers will draw their own conclusions.

To some people the idea of soliciting the opinions of writers will perhaps seem strange. What do writers know of politics and international diplomacy? they may ask. Why biographers rather than bankers, poets rather than policemen, novelists rather than newsagents? Of what particular value are their opinions? Even some of those approached voiced doubts. One contributor, though sending in his piece, argued that the days 'when writers could be expected usefully to contribute to political debates beyond the immediate sphere of their writing are altogether gone'.

The notion that authors' views are worth our attention stems from the belief that to write is, primarily, to bear witness to the truth: that the writer, of all men, has a duty not to avert his gaze from the critical issues of his day and his society. Matej Bor, the Yugoslav poet, playwright and novelist, wrote (in *Authors Take Sides on Vietnam*) that 'the writer is the conscience of the world'. And for a contributor on the Gulf War in the present collection, 'There is no other truth than the truth of the imagination'. In fact writers often invoked, sometimes quoted, other writers in making their points: their references to (among others) Virgil, Homer, Aquinas, Shakespeare, Milton, Byron, Swinburne, T.S. Eliot, Auden, Kingsley Amis, Pinter and even Bob Dylan, were clearly felt to provide a kind of authority. The writer is, generally speaking, enquiring, imaginative, rational, intellectually responsible and, above all, rarely boring. And according to Chekhov the writer's business is not to provide solutions, but to describe a situation so truthfully that the reader cannot evade it. In addition, many of the authors who responded wear more than one hat, bringing different areas of expertise to bear. They include members of the House of Commons and the House of Lords, an American ex-ambassador, a general practitioner, several economists and a number of scientists and historians.

Faced with such a wide diversity of views and approaches, we decided against the scheme adopted in *Authors Take Sides on Vietnam*, where replies were arranged more or less thematically. Our present arrangement of pieces has been kept deliberately simple. By printing them in alphabetical order we have hoped to preserve neutrality as well as ease of reference. Contributions are, with one or two exceptions, dated, since unfolding events in both conflicts undoubtedly influenced opinions. (The failure to locate weapons of mass destruction in Iraq springs to mind.)

Nevertheless, this book, like its predecessors, has many mansions. Turning its pages, the reader will realize that a significant number of those who responded regarded our two questions as merely a starting-point for a whole range of ideas. Some writers questioned the questions themselves, which in each case started by asking the recipient whether they were 'for or against' the relevant war. One author, in a covering letter, wrote that the 1991 conflict had, for him, 'illuminated the whole idea of "taking sides" and shown that this is not the way the human race ought to be thinking any more (if it wishes to preserve itself, of course)'. Twelve years later another contributor argued: 'But it isn't about taking sides'.

Even when the questions were accepted, they were not always answered. The second question in particular – 'How, in your opinion, can lasting peace be restored to the Middle East?' (1991) and 'Do you believe that the intervention will bring about lasting peace and stability in the region?' (2003) – seemed to cause problems. Many failed to answer it at all and, if they did, so indirectly that their response proved difficult to classify.

As a result, the final tally of those 'for' the 1991 and 2003 Allied actions and those 'against' must be something of an approximation. But it is possible to say that, out of the 105 responses to the Gulf War questionnaire rather more than half appear to have opposed the use of military force and out of the 71 replies to the Iraq War questionnaire, 50 were against it, a clear majority. Few in either case were neutral, though many acknowledged the problems of coming down on one side or the other. The reasons given for support or opposition were many and varied and sometimes the same arguments and criticisms were made by contributors in opposite camps and in response to both wars.

In fact, studying the contributions which follow, we are struck by the similarities of response to both conflicts, distinctive as the two were. Rather than dwelling on their areas of difference – the fact that the 1991 war was precipitated by Saddam Hussein's invasion of sovereign territory, for example, or that the Allies' response to that invasion was sanctioned by the United Nations, unlike the 2003 action – writers tend to explore what are clearly universal concerns. So that by comparing their reactions to these two different events, recurring themes begin to emerge.

The humanitarian argument, for instance, was used forcibly throughout. But while some argued that humanitarian grounds dictated that America and Britain were right to put an end to what contributors on both sides saw as Saddam's rule of terror, which included his persecution of the Kurds and Marsh Arabs, others expressed horror at the sheer scale of suffering involved in the execution of both wars; it was as bad, if not worse, they felt, than the evil it claimed to cure. As one writer in 1991 put it, 'Where there was great misery before, there is vast-scale misery now: more death, more hate, more fear'. And several writers in 2003 argued that the main casualties of the Iraq invasion, apart from priceless art treasures, were women and children, who 'don't want wars'.

It was not the only irony to emerge. Started as a fight against terrorism, it seemed to many, especially by 2003, that the Allies' action against Saddam Hussein would, if anything, increase terrorism both in the region and throughout the world. 'By invading Iraq,' one contributor wrote, 'Britain and America have handed bin Laden a priceless propaganda gift'. Few saw George W Bush's decision as helping the Israeli-Palestinian conflict, in fact many believed it was a further hindrance to a solution.

Another irony, for some, arose from the fact that, while both George Bush and Tony Blair claimed to be fighting the Iraq War from deep-seated Christian convictions, Christian leaders, including the Pope, had spoken out against it.

The notion that the 2003 war could be fought on religious grounds seemed in itself ironic to another contributor, stemming as it did from what he described as 'the arbiter of political correctness', the USA. Those who detected a racist element in the two conflicts reacted similarly. One Islamic writer deplored 'the American pilots' enjoyment in 1991 of their "turkey-shoots" and the attacks on Muslims in Western Europe'.

The greatest irony of all for some was the fact that the Western nations themselves had supplied Saddam with vast quantities of arms, biological weapons and poison gas with which to massacre his own people and wage war against neighbouring countries.

By 2003 several contributors were also pointing out the irony of a situation in which George W Bush was invading a sovereign territory for reasons other than self-defence, which was one main reason George Bush senior had given for his action against Saddam twelve years previously. As early as 1991 one author was referring to the US 'supporting, sustaining and undertaking invasions of sovereign territory: Nicaragua, East Timor, Panama' and accusing her of having supported 'a litany of tyrants: the Greek colonels, Hugo Banzer, Marcos, Duvalier, Samoza, Pinochet and d'Aubuisson'.

For some writers it was not so much a matter of irony as of hypocrisy, especially where motives were concerned. For, as even those in favour of George Bush senior's and junior's decisions observed, there were many equally worthy, if not worthier causes that could have been chosen – Tibet, Cambodia, Chile and Uganda were cited in 1991, and China, Korea and Zimbabwe in 2003. The choice of Iraq with its wealthy oilfields, it was argued, was not accidental. Those who believed that America had had vested interests in both wars found her willingness to sacrifice lives in the name of democracy particularly repugnant. While not necessarily denying the possible influence of oil in the equation, the majority view among interventionists is perhaps best summed up by the contributor who saw the 1991 war as 'part selfish oil interest and part lofty devotion to international justice'.

The concept of what does and does not constitute 'justice' occupied a number of respondents. Some took it in the legal sense. An important factor among those who believed that Saddam had to be challenged in 1991, for example, was the sanction of the United Nations, though the proviso was made that America should not be allowed to pick and choose which UN resolutions it supported. Conversely, the fact that the 2003 war failed to win the backing of the UN increased opposition to it significantly. For many writers it made the war 'illegal', with some of them going so far as to describe George W Bush and Tony Blair as guilty of 'war-crimes' and the war itself as 'a gangster act'. On the other hand, there were those who firmly believed that the UN Charter allows for military action 'if there is a humanitarian crisis' and that there had been no need for a separate resolution. Saddam himself, it was pointed out by more than one contributor, had regularly defied UN resolutions against him.

When it came to 'justice' in the broader sense, the issue was less clear-cut. While a number of writers believed that Saddam's own acts of terror justified action against him, whatever the strictly legal position, others questioned whether what they regarded as 'liberal fascism' had any right to impose a Western-style democracy in the Middle East. Some argued that sanctions and negotiations were the only acceptable route and had not been sufficiently tested. Political, not military action, they believed, was the way forward.

Then there were the pacifists, who adopted an anti-war position on principle, claiming that war solves nothing and leads only to further conflict:

'It is not bloody war but merely time that brings about change,' a 2003 contributor argued. There were also those in both conflicts who took up a pacifist stance because they believed that the particular circumstances did not justify war in the specific case under review: 'the ends do not justify the means' insisted a contributor in 2003. Another writer, referring back to the deliberate humiliating of Germany after World War I, argued that this had led directly to World War II.

The Second World War was referred to frequently. A significant number of writers invoked Hitler, whose actions, they argued, had fully justified that particular conflict. Even those opposed to the Iraq and Gulf wars often compared Saddam to Hitler, right down to his moustache, though this is contradicted by the writer who claimed that 'to compare Saddam with Hitler is to exalt Saddam and trivialize Hitler'. No one on either side attempted to defend Saddam, and his capture, while this book was being prepared for the press, will almost certainly be welcomed by the overwhelming majority of contributors.

Other unflattering comparisons for Saddam included Stalin, Milosovic, Mugabe and Napoleon. Napoleon was also conjured up by those who believed that the 1991 and 2003 conflicts had been fought to benefit the reputations of the politicians involved, on the 'Bonaparte principle' of fighting wars abroad to deflect attention from events at home. One author quoted the former Foreign Secretary, Robin Cook's charge of 10 July 2003: 'This was a war made in Washington, pushed by a handful of neo-Conservatives and pursued for reasons of US foreign strategy and domestic politics. What made this war inevitable was not an increased threat from Iraq, but a régime change in the US'. Many contributors believed that George W Bush's decision to go to war sprang directly from his need to show American voters that he was dealing with the humiliation of '9/11'. Tony Blair, according to one writer, had been merely 'drawn to the magnet of power'.

A main area of concern during both conflicts was the enormous amount of money spent on them. In the words of one contributor in 1991, the US and Britain were 'falling to pieces at home' for lack of funds for essential social services. Another reminded us that the US had 'nearly 8,000,000 homeless, millions infected with AIDS, an almost total collapse of education for blacks and a government which refuse[d] to find other forms of energy outside oil'. Famine in Africa was also mentioned. For one contributor in 2003 it was a question of 'moral priorities': Bush and Blair, he pointed out, had 'invested over two hundred billion dollars in the Iraq War, but scarcely one billion to combat the spread of Aids across Africa'.

Yet another concern of a considerable number of authors in 1991, and only slightly fewer in 2003, relates to the role of the media. Many were highly critical of what they regarded as its compliance during the fighting; the subjective way in which the war was presented; the use of jingoistic language and the suppression of impartial reporting. One writer asserted in 1991 that the war had distorted important elements in American society. That society, he believed, was developing reflexes of brutality and self-deception which could only be damaging to itself. Another contributor described the way in which the 1991 conflict was presented to the public as 'a video game to end all video games'. One writer in 2003 questioned just how 'free' the media was in the way it reported the Iraq War and several queried how 'responsible' its coverage had been.

In addition many were critical of the intelligence services, especially with regard to the question of weapons of mass destruction – WMDs, as they quickly became known. With the exception of committed pacifists, few writers doubted that WMDs ready to be deployed in 45 minutes, if found, would justify going to war in 2003. Similarly, most felt that evidence of direct links with al-Qa'ida would provide sufficient grounds. The main difference lay in those who believed both arguments had been proved and those who referred to 'non-existent' WMDs and the British government's 'dodgy dossier'. For some of the latter, the British weapons expert Dr David Kelly's suicide and the public enquiry that followed was a turning-point.

The strongest supporters of intervention, however, had no need of WMDs or proven links with al-Qa'ida to justify their convictions. One author argued that 'the single greatest impulse behind the growth of world terror has been the understanding by rogue states that the West would never fight them but always seek to buy them off in some way'. 'Morality', another writer insisted, 'does not supply political answers . . . morals are static, politics dynamic'.

When it came to the second question, about peace in the Middle East, the similarity of concerns raised is even more striking, especially given the significant time lag. Some contributors had argued in 1991 that the failure of Coalition forces to overthrow Saddam then made peace and stability in the Middle East even less likely, but most authors seemed no more hopeful about prospects there when Saddam's demise seemed inevitable in 2003. 'Are we meant to conclude that a vast demonstration of military power will scare the region into democracy, obedience and a new friendliness towards Israel?' asked one writer on 24 June 2003: 'If so, dream on.' The majority of those who replied both in 1991 and twelve years later believed that peace could only come about as a result of prolonged dialogue and negotiations between the interested parties: the main objectives, it was argued, must be a homeland for the Palestinians, in exchange for security for the Israelis and a fair deal for the Kurds.

Looking back over the past dozen years from the vantage point of the present, it would be foolish to deny that the views of some of those writing in 1991 may have changed with the unfolding situation in the Middle East, the Balkans and Eastern Europe. In fact one of the many interests of this collection is that it traces such changes among those who responded to both questionnaires, though the majority remained consistent. Even those contributing to the 2003 questions only may have already changed their views by the time they are in print, particularly in the light of Lord Hutton's Report. This book, it must be remembered, is the product of identifiable circumstances at two particular moments in time. Its purpose is to provide a contemporary record of the reactions of an articulate but not necessarily specialist section of the public from a number of countries involved.

There is, we believe, in the free discussion of problems, the identification of intransient factors of the time and region, the ingenious exploration of possibilities, the imaginative search for solutions – a permanent interest and, conceivably, a germ of hope for a less turbulent future. It is for the reader to judge whether the final result has been worthwhile.

JEAN MOORCROFT WILSON & CECIL WOOLF

Authors Take Sides on Iraq

Preface

to *Authors Take Sides on Iraq*

> 'It was adherence to the strict letter of the UN mandate that halted the US and other forces in the Gulf War [in 1991] and so left Saddam Hussein to enjoy his stolen property for another twelve years.'

This, in the opinion of one contributor to this book, marked the start of the Iraq War. It was a view shared by a number of writers.

Others date the beginnings of the war much later in November 1998 when, after seven years of sanctions and weapons inspections, Saddam ended all forms of co-operation with the United Nations Special Commission overseeing arms inspections (UNSCOM). Six weeks later, after the evacuation of UN staff from Iraq, America and Britain launched an aerial bombing campaign, 'Operation Desert Fox', to destroy what they believed to be Iraq's nuclear, chemical and biological weapons programme. In December 1999 a new UN Resolution created the Monitoring, Verification and Inspection Commission (UNMOVIC), to replace UNSCOM, and again Iraq demurred. Just over a year later, in February 2001, the US and Britain carried out further bombing raids in an attempt to disable Iraq's air defence network.

Then came the terrorist attacks on New York and Washington of 11 September 2001. The following January President Bush delivered a speech, in which he singled out Iran, Iraq and North Korea as 'an axis of evil, arming to threaten the peace of the world'. Already officials in Washington were briefing that, of the three countries of 'the axis of evil', Iraq was to be targeted for the first pre-emptive strike. But Saddam Hussein had played no known part in the '9/11' attacks on America and in the absence of any firm link between Iraq and al-Qa'ida the thinking in much of continental Europe was very different.

Tony Blair, however, seems to have been an eager participant in the struggle to overthrow Saddam. After 9/11 Blair was among the first to warn of the dangers of a 'marriage' between terrorists and rogue states developing chemical, biological and nuclear weapons. While the first priority was to destroy the Taliban and al-Qa'ida's power-base in Afghanistan, mounting pressure was put on Iraq. Tony Blair took the lead in arguing for the unconditional return of UN weapons inspectors to that country and in

March 2002 the Ministry of Defence and the Foreign Office identified Iraq as one of 'four states of concern', which were developing missile capability at the same time as seeking to acquire weapons of mass destruction.

In early September 2002 Blair flew to America for urgent talks at Camp David with George W Bush. While Downing Street officials briefed that the Prime Minister was urging the President to work through the UN, he himself played down such suggestions. Shortly afterwards, on the day following the first anniversary of the terrorist attacks, Mr Bush addressed the UN General Assembly. Returning to the theme of the axis of evil, he said, 'By seeking weapons of mass destruction, these regimes pose a grave and gathering danger'. He added that he 'would not wait on events while dangers gather . . . So we must act pre-emptively to ensure that those who have that capability aren't allowed to proliferate it'. Washington, he said, wanted to work through the Security Council, but military action would be unavoidable if Iraq failed to comply with UN resolutions.

Twelve days later, Parliament was recalled from its long summer recess for an emergency debate on the growing crisis over Iraq. Blair set out the case for military action to disarm Saddam, notably that the policy of sanctions and no-fly zones enforced by Britain and America was no longer working; that Iraq's WMD programme was not shut down, but 'up and running'. To coincide with this crucial debate in September 2002, the Government published a 50-page dossier, setting out previously secret intelligence material, purporting to detail Iraq's attempts to acquire nuclear weapons and develop long-range missiles. Saddam Hussein, it was claimed, had WMDs ready to be deployed in 45 minutes. In the meantime, the British Government was working to get the UN to set Iraq a final deadline to disarm and demonstrate to Saddam that the international community was in earnest.

On 8 November 2002 the Security Council passed Resolution 1441, calling on Iraq to abandon all weapons of mass destruction and threatening 'serious consequences' if it failed to comply. Iraq accepted the terms of the resolution and UN weapons inspectors were allowed back into the country. On 12 December the Iraqi Government sent the UN a 12,000-page document, claiming it was a complete declaration of all its chemical, biological, nuclear and missile programmes. The Americans said the declaration was incomplete and declared Iraq to be in 'material breach' of Resolution 1441. Tony Blair was equally dismissive and accused Baghdad of lying about its weapons capability. He then embarked on a strenuous and futile attempt to secure a second UN resolution setting a final deadline for Saddam.

At the end of January 2003, Bush and Blair met to agree a timetable for military action. In early March, however, President Chirac declared that France would oppose any resolution that authorized the use of force. Mr Blair was facing growing opposition from his own party, his colleagues in the Cabinet and throughout the country. In Washington the Defence Secretary Donald Rumsfeld talked of America going to war without Britain, because of Blair's domestic difficulties. The Prime Minister told his critics it was too late to back down. Bush and Blair met in the Azores on 16 March 2003 to finalize plans for the invasion of Iraq. The House of Commons debated the issue on 18 March and despite a rebellion by 139 Labour MPs, Blair won convincingly and two days later military action began.

More than 400,000 US troops and 45,000 British troops were sent to Iraq, with 2,000 Australian troops. The war lasted 26 days, from the bombing of Baghdad on 20 March to the coalition declaring control of every major city in Iraq and 'major combat operations' over on 14 April. Nine months later Saddam Hussein has been captured and the occupying forces are still meeting significant resistance and suffering casualties. Both in Britain and America the main protagonists are coming under increasing pressure to justify their decision to take their countries to war.

Our questionnaire was sent out to authors over a period of six months from 5 May to mid-November 2003, asking two questions:

Were you for, or against, the American-led military action against Saddam Hussein's regime in March 2003?
Do you believe that the intervention will bring about lasting peace and stability in the region?

The Answers

The Questions

Were you for, or against, the American-led military action against Saddam Hussein's regime in March 2003?

Do you believe that the intervention will bring about lasting peace and stability in the region?

The Answers

Dannie Abse

Bring your TV cameras, bring your microphones.
Soldier to the broad gate, soldiers to the fire.
Oblivion is their name, vultures to their bones,
While far behind, with proper melancholy,
The ineffectual poet strums his lyre.

14 July 2003

Brian Aldiss

A connection between Saddam Hussein and the events of 9/11 in New York was always evident but somewhat obscure. While sympathizing with the Americans for the devastating blow they suffered, I was offended by President George Bush's announcement that there was to be a War waged of Good against Evil. Such moral terms seemed inappropiate, more suitable for the fictions of J.R.R. Tolkien than for geopolitics; honesty would have admitted it was more a struggle of the Rich against the Poor.

It was this statement of the President's that, more than anything, contributed to a marked lack of enthusiasm for what followed: for going to war against Iraq (or against Saddam, whichever way you wish to phrase it).

This has been a war which, for the people of the West, has been delivered to us largely by such media as television and radio. Just before the invasion, various British television channels, in particular Channel 4 and the BBC channels, devoted several excellent programmes showing us the lives of ordinary Iraqis and the ancient treasures contained within the territory of Iraq and its museums. It was impressive to see ordinary people making the best of things, being charming and pleasant, visiting tea-rooms, and (in one case) reading a daily newspaper which showed a photo of David Beckham on its front cover.

These were the lives and relics which were to be put in jeopardy by the forces of the USA and the UK—forces not greatly reckoned to have particularly vivid insight into, or veneration for, Iraqi life and history.

All this is to say that one holds a concern for the sanctity of everyday life in particular, and a general mistrust for the brutality of war in general.

Nevertheless, set against that, Saddam Hussein had regularly defied UN motions against him, and we heard this repeated assertion that Saddam had WMD which could be, so we gathered, unleashed against the West in 45 minutes. Why did we find this credible at the time? Mainly because of the unsuspected violence which had been unleashed only recently against New York. In that sense, and knowing that Saddam was a murderous tyrant, one acceded to government statements that war was necessary.

Your second question is more difficult to answer. It's the adjective 'lasting' which creates the difficulty. How long is lasting? However, we may suppose that a sort of peace and a sort of stability can be plugged into the Iraq community, if the community will allow it. British troops after deciding they would not shell ancient Basra shelled ancient Basra. That was an argument of necessity. Our reputations have suffered in consequence. There is no doubt that Western armies have caused much damage and disruption; but to a great extent the Iraqi people themselves have inflicted considerable damage on their own infrastructure, in their first mad days of 'freedom'. However, repairs go ahead, we understand, water and electrical systems are being reinstalled, and we can hope that everyone will slowly calm down.

You might have asked a third question: Do Western powers have some sort of inalienable right to interfere in the policies, however obnoxious, of other less privileged nations of the world?

Our present uncertainties are compounded by such enigmas as the role of the UN, and the characters of such leading players as George Bush and Tony Blair. Or are we merely witnessing another demonstration of the truth of Lord Byrons's verse (in *Childe Harold's Pilgrimage*):

> This makes the madmen who have made men mad
> By their contagion; conquerors and kings,
> Founders of sects and systems, to whom add
> Sophists, bards, statesmen, all unquiet things
> Which stir too strongly the soul's secret springs,
> And are themselves the fools to those they fool;
> Envied, yet how unenviable! What stings
> Are theirs! One breast laid open were a school
> Which would unteach mankind the lust to shine or rule.

10 July 2003

John Arden

When we claim there's a good reason for going to war we always put forward the most reputable motives — e.g. the defence of ourselves (and others) against violence and tyranny. We tend not to make much of the *dis*reputable motives (which may nonetheless be equally strong): greed, fear, revenge, hatred of other people's *difference*. Those who oppose going to war will naturally list all its horrors, and indeed have done so since the days of Homer; but it is an argument that has never, in practical terms, convinced. The men who laid Troy waste knew what would happen to the Trojans, the men who dropped cluster bombs all over Afghanistan knew what would happen to the children who picked them up, and yet they still did it – they believed they had no alternative. An appeal to compassion doesn't work: the Ends, it is always said, justify the Means.

No, they don't.

I prefer to say that the Means *determine* the Ends. One war makes another, and no victory is ever complete, no violent solution can ever resolve violence. A simplified summary: — World War I bred World War 2; World War 2 bred the Cold War with its offspring in Korea and Vietnam; World War 2 also bred the Israel/Palestine War; Vietnam bred the Gulf War, a superficially easy triumph to smother the memory of a painful defeat; Israel/Palestine, combined with the Gulf War, bred 11 September, the Afghan War, and the assault upon Iraq.

If this were properly understood, war would cease to be regarded as a normal item of national policy. Or would be if our rulers were guided by rational principle. But of course they never are. Convinced that Ends justify Means, they work always for the short-term advantage; and war – in the short term – most certainly brings advantages. For the rulers, that is to say: not necessarily for the ruled. But the ruled can too often be persuaded, cajoled, seduced, intimidated, coerced, into believing that they also have something to gain from the slaughterhouse prepared for them.

Just look at the state of a world where war is a 'normal item'. More than $900 billion per year is spent on military budgets, half of it by the United States alone. Only 10% of this would ensure the essentials of life for the entire planet, devastated though much of it is by starvation and disease. Women and children are the majority of victims of armed conflict, comprise 80% of refugees and displaced people, and are killed and maimed by landmines long after conflicts end. Yet women, as one-half of the human race, are routinely expected to supply all-round care and succour throughout and after the war (*care and succour without which no war would be possible*); their work, on a worldwide basis, is neither recognized, assessed nor paid for.* They are expected to do it for love and the sense of duty. Soldiers too are called to their duty: but if they are to fight, they need to be paid. Armament-mongers need to be paid for the weapons they supply. Oil-mongers need to be paid for their oil. (War needs oil. Oil needs war. Blood and oil, the warriors' broth of the new millennium.) And of course, rulers need to be paid: not only in money, but adulation and power.

I have always been an admirer of the United States and its traditions of democracy and civil liberty. At present, however, from the far side of the Atlantic, I see a nation that has somehow slipped under the repressive control of a gang of oil-mongers, enron-rats, vote-fakers, environment-foulers, abhorrers of any sort of liberty or democratic practice from which they themselves cannot suck gravy. Even before 11 September with all its horrors, this crew had made it clear that they were also essentially war-mongers, because without war their cormorant-greed must implode through its own incompetence. They received from the hands of the al-Qa'ida fanatics the very pretext they looked for. I must not forget to add: *they made their war despite the protests of thousands upon thousands of honourable US citizens.*

The government of Great Britain (my own country) contrived to get sucked into the maelstrom; while the government of Ireland (where I live) cravenly opened its airports for a war that clearly horrifies it.

The above was my view before March 2003. I have not changed my mind because Saddam has been toppled, or because the casualties were not as great as many of us feared, or because the evidence of Saddam's atrocities is even stronger than it was before. I do not believe that the Near East and Middle East are in any way 'stabilized' by the war. The Israel/Palestine problem remains as it always was; the al-Qa'ida problem is perhaps even worse than it was; and Iraq (as also Afghanistan) seems to have been freed from the clutches of tyranny only to be given over to a deadly combination of indigenous war-lords and western carpet-baggers.

**How many know that a United Nations resolution, No. 1325, in 2000, called for women to be included in all aspects of peace-making and peace-building discussions? It was passed unanimously: to what extent any government or paramilitary organization bears it in mind (let alone implements it) is anybody's guess.*

16 May 2003

Beryl Bainbridge

I was against the attack on Iraq, not because of any considered understanding of the reasons for such a conflict, rather because I lean towards the belief that wars have been waged for centuries and that victory has never been of any use to the dead. I also believe that Saddam Hussein was bound to die sooner or later, and that, judging by press reports, his successors were too demented, drugged and diseased to hold onto power for very long. As the Americans and ourselves have reportedly been bombing Iraq for the last twelve years, I couldn't imagine why it would be necessary to stage an invasion.

My own experience of war, that of England against Hitler, in which the death toll came to 55 million, was played out during my childhood in Liverpool. I carried a gas-mask to school, and when the air-raid sirens sounded, filed in crocodile to the shelters in the dug-up hockey field. At night, my brother and I were put to bed under the dining room table.

We had a picture of Marshal Stalin on our kitchen wall. My father said Uncle Joe was the saviour of the world. I was introduced in the Khardomah Café to a man called Mr Gerhart, who had fled Germany in 1938. He had a dent in his forehead where he'd been hit for being Jewish. Mr Gerhart said the war was being fought because the Nazis wanted to wipe out the Jews.

I kept a diary in 1942—there are only two entries:

2nd September 1942, The Germans kill 50,000 Jews in Warsaw Ghetto. Daddy upset.

18th September. *Battle of Stalingrad. Uncle Joe worried not a bit.*

Five years later, on the 18th July, a ship named the *Exodus* carrying 5,000 survivors of the Holocaust to the port of Haifa was attacked by British troops and forced to return to Cyprus. Twenty years later my children came home from school and told me Joe Stalin was a monster, the equal of Hitler.

Since then people have blown one another to pieces in Vietnam, Korea, Libya, Ireland, Britain, the Falklands, Kosovo, Bosnia, America, Burma, Egypt, Russia, Iran, Palestine, Africa, Israel and Iraq.

In the last two decades methods of war have undergone a change. Hand to hand fighting has gone out of fashion and it is no longer acceptable that soldiers should die in battle. With the invention of smart bombs, murder is now best committed from a great height.

I have no idea whether the recent conflict will lead to peace or stability. Why should it? Judging by the lessons of history, it is not bloody war but merely time that brings about change.

5 May 2003

Julian Barnes

The reasons put forward by the British government to justify the Anglo-American invasion were at best flimsy, at worst mendacious. The British 'dossier' was feeble and plagiaristic; the American presentation to the UN astonishingly thin. Finally, when these justifications seemed insufficient, the humanitarian argument was invoked, a sudden, hypocritical rush to caring where little had previously been evidenced.

We went to war because America had already decided to go to war for – unsurprisingly — American reasons (9/11, Bush family history, oil, military cojones). The nearest the government came to admitting this was when Jack Straw said Europe would 'reap the whirlwind' if America went in alone: a pathetic and morally inept line of reasoning.

Lasting peace and stability? American and British military occupation of an Arab country is a great free advertisement for terror groups generally. Nor is America likely to arrange elections which Islamists might win. As for the Israel-Palestine question, if the best chance of a solution is US diplomatic muscle, why could that not have been applied without a war? Or are we meant to conclude that a vast demonstration of military power will scare the region into democracy, obedience and a new friendliness towards Israel? If so, dream on.

24 June 2003

Correlli Barnett

Before the war I consistently opposed in various newspapers the American drive towards an attack on Iraq, on the score that a) no evidence of Weapons of Mass Destruction, or of an imminent threat to Great Britain, had been proved; and b) that the American aim of 'regime change' would represent an unprovoked aggression against a sovereign state, and hence a breach of the UN Charter. After the event, this still remains my position, especially since *no* evidence of WMD has been discovered.

I do *not* believe that the American conquest and occupation of Iraq (abetted by Tony Blair) will bring lasting peace and stability to the Middle East. We already see that the promise of 'liberating' the Iraqis and bringing them democracy has in reality become an American imperial takeover, with an American viceroy ruling through appointed Iraqi puppets. We see that Iraqi oil sales will be used by the Americans to enrich American main contractors who will repair the damage inflicted by American bombs and missiles. Arab and Islamic resentment of United States hegemony has been enhance, not diminished.

As for wider implications for 'stability', we see the Americans using their new main Middle-East military base in Iraq as the platform for uttering threats against Syria and Iran. As for the 'road map' towards an Israeli-Palestinian peace settlement, it is virtually certain that *no* compromise acceptable to both parties can ever be agreed. The terminal blockages on 'the road map' are likely to be supplied by the issue of Jerusalem and the power of the Jewish lobby in American politics.

2 June 2003

Tony Benn

America invaded, conquered and occupied Iraq to get the oil and dominate the region.

Bush tore up the Charter of the UN and is busy building the biggest Empire the world has ever known.

The reasons given were fraudulent and the world was against it.

Britain, by going along with it may have been guilty of war crimes and we will all have to pay a price for it.

I was against the war and still am.

5 May 2003

Louis Bolliet

I am entirely against the American-led military action against Iraq. Only the United Nations should make such a decision.

I do not believe that this intervention will bring about lasting peace and stability in the region. I anticipate great suffering for the people and continuing instability in the Middle East.

24 October 2003

Pascal Boniface

I was against the American war in Iraq. Of course I strongly opposed the Saddam regime, hoping that the Iraqi people would be liberated from it. But, in any case, I was not convinced by the American arguments. Washington had been comfortable with this regime for years. It was not the only dictatorship in the world. The official arguments – WMD and democracy – appeared to be fake. The real one, geopolitical interests, was never said. I opposed the doctrine of so-called pre-emptive self-defence, which seemed to be a new form of strong-arm tactics. Besides that, it was illogical and dangerous to attack Iraq in the name of international law while neither saying nor doing anything about the Israeli occupation of Palestine.

The present situation proves only that winning a war is easier than winning the peace, and that in a globalized world even the sole hyperpower is unable to control against its will a poor and looted nation of 23 million people.

17 September 2003

Gordon Bowker

I am not a pacifist. If the argument had been that Saddam Hussein was a filthy torturer and mass murderer and the United Nations could not stand by and allow his atrocities to continue, and that all other such dictators could expect the same, I would have been well able to support an invasion.

But the main reason given by Tony Blair was so clearly trumped up that one could only suspect that the true motive was an ignoble one, and, from the point of view of the troops involved, a cynical deception. It doesn't help that the prime movers in this case lack credibility at just about every level imaginable. Eliot's lines from *Murder in the Cathedral* make the ethical point most succinctly:

The last temptation is the greatest treason:
To do the right deed for the wrong reason.

So, an honest statement of intention, backed by honest reasons, articulated by honest politicians would probably have won me over – and many other doubters besides.

Needless to say, it is good that a monster like Saddam has gone from power. But who can be confident that the conquering powers will prevent one menace being replaced by yet another? And in the meantime, the other monsters continue to murder and shovel over the mass graves unabashed.

Of course, if weapons of mass destruction are verifiably unearthed in Iraq, I and a few others will have to eat our words. But somehow, it seems unlikely.

9 December 2003

Alan Brownjohn

Against. But why just American-*led*? It was American-*conceived*, American-*scheduled* and, for the most part, American-*executed* – though substituting 'Bush' for 'American' and adding 'blessed by Blair' throughout might be fairer. And then, why only 'in March and April 2003'? There has been continuous action against Iraq, through sanctions and bombing, since the end of the Gulf War of 1991, though it hasn't always made the headlines. As much suffering in Iraq has been caused by external action as by Saddam's tyranny, possibly more; which is not to minimise, let alone excuse, the horrors of Saddam's tyranny, simply recognise that what the West was doing merely served to reinforce it. The same kind of folly over Kosovo hardened the attitude of Slobodan Milosevic , and in that sense both men were the creations of American policy.

Here is a piece of advice for all poor, unprotected, decent people in the world: Don't live in a country where oil (Iraq) or minerals (Kosovo) will tempt American or European invaders, because they will find wonderful moral justifications for grabbing it – as I write, American corporations are systematically moving in on Iraq's resources and utilities. Oh, and don't have an infrastructure of industry, transport, hospitals, etc. within tempting range of construction companies who will move in to repair what the bombers have destroyed and then charge you for the favour.

It would be obvious just to respond [to your second question]'No, of course not, it hasn't so far and it won't in the future'. But things are more complicated than that. Unpredictability is what Middle Eastern history is about. For instance, there *could* emerge as a result of this war an even more brutal, and yes, stable, fundamentalist tyranny over wide swathes of the region than anything the more secular Saddam Hussein ever organized. That might be represented as 'peace' of a certain kind, and I would expect America rapidly to do business there, much as it did originally with Saddam. It knows where the gasolene is, and wants it. On the other hand, an ongoing, bloody, draining sort of guerilla war and continuing international terrorism seems more likely. *Most* likely is a combination of both, with America pretending that peace and stability has been achieved, as in Afghanistan. This is where the hollow, mendacious and self-righteous leaders of Britain and the United States have led their peoples. It makes an innocent faith in the power and propriety of Western democracy and its freedoms – including its 'free' media –look callow and irresponsible.

1 October 2003

Helen Bryan

The moral high ground is widely accessible, and one need not be an author to prefer peace to armed conflict. I supported military intervention in Iraq as a last resort, and continue to do so, though I wish there had been a viable alternative. Like the Bible-belt preacher who, asked to define his position on sin, replied briefly, 'I'm agin it,' I am 'agin' war. Reality, however, is less simple.

In case the world needed reminding, the maxim 'all evil requires to flourish is for good people to do nothing' was graphically illustrated when nothing was done to prevent the wholesale massacre of Tutsis in Rwanda, the slaughter of Muslims in the United Nations' 'safe haven' of Sebrenica, or the streets of Sierra Leone running with blood, to name but a few recent consequences of collective inaction. Unless abstract principles of the value of human life, the merits of democracy and freedom, a desire for universal peace, justice and human rights or the evils of war can be given practical effect in the real world, they are about as relevant as medieval theologians' impassioned discussions about the number of angels able to dance on the head of a pin. The Four Horsemen of the Apocalypse will not pause mid-headlong rush for reflection because nice folk wave placards for peace. The American-led military action in Iraq is an inevitable consequence of United Nations' cumulative dithering in the face of Saddam Hussein's refusal to comply with United Nations resolutions since the end of the Gulf War.

Emotion, however refined, deeply felt, or eloquently expressed is rarely a substitute for a grasp of the facts. Anti-war marchers protesting 'not in my name' in Hyde Park and demanding the United Nations, the weapons inspectors and Peace to be given a chance might have gone home glowing and validated in their idealism, but they should take a closer look at the United Nations' record.

In the case of Iraq, Saddam Hussein's reign of terror, genocide, human rights abuses, torture, and the threat posed to the region and the world by a military dictatorship whose past development of a nuclear capacity, chemical weapons, and readiness to invade a neighbouring state, are a matter of record. Bleats that the United States once found him an ally are neither here nor there at this stage. However regrettable, that issue has been superseded by more immediate considerations, which those opposing the war have not addressed adequately, convincingly or at all. Yet there is a huge body of information on events leading up to the present conflict, easily available on the Internet on sites such as www.iraqwatch.com. This site is a good starting point, and highlights the astonishing failure of the UN in Iraq. Hamstrung by bureaucracy, defective procedures, and the appointment of Hans Blix as chief weapons inspector, referred to by the *Wall Street Journal* as 'Hans the Timid' and later 'Hans the Irrelevant', the sole non-military force that might have been effective, was not. The catalogue of UN failures left a vacuum to be exploited by Saddam Hussein, and exploited it was.

Whether military intervention will prove to bring stability and a lasting peace depends on many factors, but to turn the question around, the prospects of stability and lasting peace in the region seemed marginal to non-existent and worse under Saddam Hussein. His removal was a necessary precondition, and his capture by the Americans has eliminated that threat.

15 December 2003

Jilly Cooper

I was utterly against the war in Iraq. I felt it was completely unjustified and just motivated by an American desire to dominate the Middle East and secure control of the oil. I fail to see why Saddam has to be removed at such colossal expense and loss of life and destruction to Iraq and Mugabe is left to carry on his murderous regime.

I think the British Army was a credit to us and fought wonderfully well, but a musician friend of mine, who teaches the bands of one of the most important regiments, said the soldiers when they came back, absolutely loathed being there. They didn't feel they were fighting, as they were in the Falklands, for anything necessary, and were reduced to the role of stretcher-bearers, carrying the limbs and bodies of Iraqi women and children to be buried.

The terrifying thing was that with so much coverage on television, there was an awful, sick craving to know what was going on. I was horrified to find myself quite excited at times – just as I would be when my favourite team won a football match. Although the television correspondents were absolutely heroic. But there again, far too many of them were killed, as far too many people died from 'friendly fire'.

8 May 2003

Jim Crace

It was never likely that the violent overthrow of a regime with base standards by a couple of governments with double standards would add much to the gaiety of nations.

18 June 2003

Andy Croft

Were you for, or against, the American-led military intervention against Saddam Hussein's regime in March and April 2003?

Against. It's clear those unconvincing lies
Re WMDs were just designed
To make a quite illegal enterprise
Seem necessary in the public mind
(And now of course to everyone's surprise
They're proving rather difficult to find!)
In war the USA's the market-leader,
The claim that they are on some new crusade
Against a gruesome crew called Al-Qaida,
They somehow think permits them to invade
Just where and when they want to, gentle reader.
Such double-talk should make us all afraid.
If this old dirty world is getting grubbier
It's thanks to lying crooks like Blair and Dubya.

Do you believe that the intervention will bring about lasting peace and stability in the region?

The history of the region offers ample
Instruction on the benefits of war
When superpowers are allowed to trample
Without restraint on international law
(Afghanistan's a pretty good example
Of how such wars leave poor folk just as poor).
Instead of MAD – which means that in the name of self-defence
We've now the doctrine of Pre-emptive Strike,
Which means that in the name of self-defence
We bomb to bits small countries we don't like

Whose governments have given us offence
(The model seems to be the old Third Reich).
But History shows we never come off worst
Because we always hit the bullies first.

9 September 2003

Anthony Curtis

I grew up to manhood in the 1930s. As a Jewish-born English schoolboy I read accounts and saw on newsreels the spectacle of race-hatred pursued as the official government policy of a nation-state. I met and came to know well some of the children in my peer-group who had been fortunate enough to escape from its more lethal consequences. Bewildered, I observed the tacit acceptance of race-hatred by other nation states unwilling to condemn it out of hand or combat it until it threatened their own security. The experience of this passive attitude by those in power has left me with a deep gut-approval of any positive action taken to eliminate the perpetrators of race-hatred.

My approval was, therefore, immediately aroused by the declaration of war against Saddam Hussein and his regime. On reflection, after the first shock of realizing that, yes, there really was going to be another war, the rational mind dreaded what this would entail. After the war had begun, I agonised (from the safety of my television set) over the bombing, the devastation, the loss and maiming of innocent lives. But all that has come to light of Saddam's regime, and the behaviour of the Ba'ath Party during his dictatorship, has only served to confirm and strengthen my initial sense of approval.

28 May 2003

Richard Dawkins

I write this on the eve of war, haunted by my countryman W.H. Auden's lines on 1 September 1939:

I sit in one of the dives
On fifty-second street
Uncertain and afraid
As the clever hopes expire . . .

I know that what I say can make no difference – will anyway be overtaken by events before it is published. All I can attempt is the long view.

Whether or not the war has nominally ended by the time you read this, it will not be the end. The Islamic world will be plunged into a seething stew of humiliated resentment, from which generations of 'martyrs' will rise, led by new Osamas. The scars of enmity between Britain and her erstwhile friends in Europe may take years to heal. NATO may never recover. As for the UN, quite apart from the corrupt spectacle of the world's leading power bribing and bullying small countries to hand over their votes, it is mortally wounded. The fragile semblance of a rule-of-law in international affairs, painstakingly built up since World War II, is collapsing.. A precedent is set for any country to attack any other country they happen to dislike and are strong enough to defeat. Who knows how this precedent may play itself out, if followed by North Korea, Israel, Pakistan or India, countries which really *do* have weapons of mass destruction?

Osama bin Laden, in his wildest dreams, could hardly have hoped for this. A mere eighteen months after he boosted the United States to a peak of worldwide sympathy and popularity unprecedented since Pearl Harbor, the totality of that international goodwill has been squandered to near zero. Bin Laden must be beside himself with glee. And, Allah be praised, the infidels are now walking right into the Iraq trap.

There was always a risk for bin Laden that his attacks on New York and Washington might raise world sympathy for the United States, thereby thwarting his long-term aim of holy war against the Great Satan. He needn't have worried. With the Bush junta at the helm, a camel could have foreseen the outcome. And the beauty is that it doesn't matter what happens in the war. Imagine how it looks from bin Laden's warped point of view:

If the American victory is swift, Bush will have done our work for us, removing the hated Saddam Hussein with his secular, un-Islamic ways, and opening the way for a decent theocracy ruled by Ayatollahs or Talibanis. Even better, as a war 'hero' the strutting, swaggering Bush may actually win an election. Who can guess what he will then get up to, and what resentments he will arouse, when he finally has something to swagger about? We shall have so many martyrs volunteering, we shall run out of targets. Or, if the American victory is slow and bloody, things might be better still. Admittedly, Bush will probably fall in 2004 and Saddam be seen as a martyr, but never mind. The hatred that a prolonged war generates will set us up for the foreseeable future, even if the Americans elect a less gloriously useful President. How could we have hoped for more?

A handful of the zealous faithful, mostly Saudis with a few Egyptians, armed only with box-cutters and deep religious faith, simultaneously commandeered four large airliners and flew three of them, undisturbed by fighter aircraft or – mysteriously – by any immediate government attention at all, into large buildings with catastrophic loss of life. Praise be to Allah. But mark the sequel. It is almost too good to be true but, as a direct consequence of this attack, the entire might of the United States Army, Navy and Air Force is diverted away from us, and hurled at a completely different country, whose only connection with 9/11 is that its people belong to the same 'race' and religion as our glorious martyrs.

Whatever anyone may say about weapons of mass destruction, or about Saddam's savage brutality to his own people, the reason Bush can now get away with his war is that a sufficient number of Americans see it as *revenge* for 9/11. This is not only bizarre. It is pure racism and/or religious prejudice, given that nobody has made even a faintly plausible case that Iraq had anything to do with the atrocity. It was Arabs that hit the World Trade Center, right? So let's go and kick Arab ass. Those 9/11 terrorists were Muslims, right? Right. And Iraqis are Muslims, right? Right. That does it.

The official reasons for this war were equally applicable before 9/11, and before the last election. Yet, though it has certainly lurked, ever since the first Gulf War, in the dark minds of some of the men behind Bush, it never got a mention in his election manifesto, nor in that of his stooge Blair. Indeed, of all major world leaders, only Gerhard Schroder has put the war to an electorate –he was against it – and consequently he could claim to be the only one with a democratic mandate for what he is now doing.

As for my own country, even the minority who support Tony Blair's pro-Bush policy do so with the minimum of enthusiasm. Max Hastings is a veteran newspaper editor with a stalwart reputation, dating back even before the Falklands war, as a right-wing hawk on most issues. If anybody among British opinion-formers could have been expected to stand with Bush, it is Max Hastings. In the *Telegraph*, Britain's most consistently right-wing newspaper, Hastings has written a remarkable piece which is worth quoting:

> 'Some of us have always argued that this is not a crisis about handling Iraq –it is about how the rest of the world manages the US. Our only superpower possesses the means to impose its will anywhere, without military aid from anyone. It is vital that allies should dissuade the US from pursuing a unilateral foreign policy, which is why I, for one, reluctantly support British participation in the war . . .'

Hastings explains how Tony Blair's desperate efforts to salvage some sort of respectability in international law were fatally undermined by the Bush Administration's transparent intention to go to war whatever happened, following a pre-determined military timetable,

> 'This was an irresistible invitation for others, notably the French, to throw the toys out of the pram. Mr Bush and his colleagues have casually insulted half the globe . . . Watching [Donald Rumsfeld] in diplomatic action reminds one of an elephant taking a stroll in a Japanese bonsai garden . . .'

Hastings hopes for a swift American victory which will leave the world 'a marginally better place without Saddam'. But . . .

> 'Mr Bush has achieved the near-impossible, by creating an international constituency for Saddam. Heaven help us; if he persists with his doctrine of the rightness of might after capturing Baghdad, he could build a coalition in support of Kim Jong Il.'

Bush seems sincerely to see the world as a battleground between Good and Evil (the capital letters are deliberate). It is Us against Them, St Michael's angels against the forces of Lucifer. We shall smoke out the Amalekites, send a posse after the Midianites, smite them all and let God deal with their souls. Some of Bush's faithful supporters even welcome war as the necessary prelude to Armageddon and the Rapture. We must presume, or at least hope, that Bush himself is not quite of that bonkers persuasion. But he really does seem to believe he is wrestling, on God's behalf, against some sort of disembodied spirit of Evil.

Evil (like 'Sin' and like 'Terror', Bush's favourite target before the current Iraq distraction) is not an entity, not a spirit, not a force to be opposed and subdued. Evil is a collection of nasty things that nasty people do. There are nasty people in every country, stupid people, insane people, people who, for all sorts of reasons, should never be allowed to get anywhere near power. Just killing nasty people doesn't help: they will simply be replaced. We must try to tailor our institutions, our constitutions, our electoral systems, so as to minimize the chance that they will rise to the top. In the case of Saddam Hussein, we in the west must bear some guilt. The United States, Britain and France have all, from time to time, done our bit to shore up Saddam and even arm him.

And let us look to our own vaunted democratic institutions. The population of the United States is nearly 300 million, including many of the best-educated, most talented, most resourceful, most ingenious, most humane people on earth. By almost any measure of civilized attainment, from Nobel Prize-counts on down, the United States leads the world by miles. You would think that a country with such resources, and such a field of talent, would be able to devise a constitution and an electoral procedure that would ensure a leadership of the highest quality. Yet, what has happened? At the end of all the Primaries and Party Caucuses, after all the speeches and the televized debates, after a year or more of non-stop electioneering bustle and balloons and razzamatazz, who, out of that entire population of 300 million, has emerged at the top of the heap? George W Bush.

Those of us who marched through London, a million strong, to oppose Tony Blair's craven support for the Iraq war, are sometimes accused of anti-Americanism. I vigorously repudiate the charge. I am strongly pro-American, which is one reason I am passionately anti-Bush. You didn't elect him. You deserve better, and so do the rest of us. Even if the Florida vote wasn't deliberately rigged, Al Gore's majority in the country, reinforcing his majority in the Electoral College but for dead-heated Florida, should have led a just and unpartisan Supreme Court to award the tie-breaker to him. Bush came to power by what I can only, if oxymoronically, call a constitutional *coup d'état.*

Forgive my presumption, but could it just be that there is something a teeny weeny bit wrong with that famous US constitution? Is it really a good idea, for example, that a single person's vote, buried deep within the margin of error for a whole State, can by itself swing a full 25 votes in the Electoral College, one way or the other? And is it really sensible that money should translate itself so directly and transparently into electoral success, so that a successful candidate must either be very rich or prepared to sell favours to those who are? Would you do business with a company that devoted an entire year to little else than head-hunting its new CEO, from the strongest field in the world, and ended up with George W Bush? Think about it, guys.

14 May 2003

Louis de Bernières

In principle I am in favour of forcibly deposing all stalinist and fascist regimes, and establishing democracies in their place. My parents' generation did this on our behalf, and we owe them eternal thanks. In this case it is a shame that Weapons of Mass Destruction were used as a pretext, especially if they turn out to have been illusory. If they do turn out to be illusory, and I was Tony Blair, I would put a gun to my head and shoot myself out of sheer embarrassment.

Arabs have no natural tradition of democracy, and their religion gives them an ultra-conservative, patriarchal, authoritarian and absolutist cast of mind. I fear that in Iraq they will simply vote to abolish democracy and create an Islamic state, in which case deposing Saddam Hussein would have been fairly pointless. The alternative would be an unelected American-supervised puppet regime, which is not what we were fighting for.

The intervention will no doubt have served as a salutary warning to various surrounding states, but there will be no peace and stability in the region until the Israelis feel secure and have given up Nazi tactics such as driving people off their land and creating ghettoes. A Palestinian state has to be established, and Arabs in general must democratize, get educated, and stop blaming everyone else for their own mess-ups. I look forward to the day when every synagogue and every mosque has become a concert hall or a cinema. All this is to say that peace and stability are unlikely to happen in the region for a very long time, because none of the above are likely to come about. Western countries should make urgent efforts to stop sourcing their energy from that region, so that we have as little to do with them as possible. I might point out that most of the troubles in the region derive from the Western powers' dismemberment of the Ottoman Empire, which for centuries had preserved the peace by sitting heavily and impartially on everyone. Are we really prepared to do that in our turn?

16 June 2003

Margaret Drabble

I was against the military action against Saddam Hussein's regime, because it was undertaken without an international mandate and it threatens international law. It suggests a dangerous trend of creeping American imperialism, also illustrated by the detaining of so-called illegal combatants without charge in Guantanamo Bay. The war was inadequately justified, and the justifications for it have kept changing in recent months. A very dangerous precedent has been created.

I doubt if the intervention will bring peace and lasting stability in the region, though if it does, I will eat some of my words. It seems to me more likely that it will further de-stabilize the region, and that we may see a tragic situation develop like that in Algeria, where the death toll has been very high. The intervention is perceived as an attack by the richest in the world on the poorest in the world. This is not very surprising and does not augur well. It is clear that the Americans will not tolerate a regime that does not suit them and their interests, and it is not clear how such a regime will legitimately emerge.

9 June 2003

Duncan Fallowell

Militant Islam is the totalitarianism of the 21st century. It has shut down the life of the mind in its own countries and is seeking to do the same to ours. Unless we are prepared to succumb to a new Dark Age, the west has no alternative but to confront militant Islam in its various secular and religious forms. As for a lasting peace in the region, well, the Middle East has been a nightmare since the end of the Ottoman Empire. It has all but choked to death on the three gruesome religions which have been its tragic legacy to the world: Judaism, Christianity, Islam. It is kept going on a life support system of petrodollars. The only hope for the Middle East is to shut off this vast stream of money from the west by finding an alternative to oil. The region might then sink back into a relatively tranquil world of date palms, desert sunsets and kif.

8 June 2003

Anne Fine

1. Against.
2. No.

3 June 2003

Robert Fisk

Just before the illegal Anglo-American invasion of Iraq, I purchased a copy of Lieutenant-General Sir Stanley Maude's 1917 proclamation to the people of Baghdad. 'We come here not as conquerors but as liberators,' he told the supposedly 'liberated' people of the Iraqi capital after the British invasion in the Great War, '. . . to rid you from generations of tyranny.'

I had already mentioned the existence of this remarkable document in *The Independent*, and it was a sign of the times – and of my financial misfortune – that by the time I could bid for General Maude's proclamation, my paper's readers flocked to the same auction and put the price up from £250 to £1,750. They realized – like so many others in Britain – that history was about to repeat itself, based on a foundation of lies and deceit.

Indeed, I don't think that mendacity – by both the British and American governments – has ever been quite so brazen. The so-called 'dossiers' of evidence which Tony Blair distributed to 'prove' that Saddam Hussein was concealing weapons of mass destruction had been rumbled and exposed for the pack of forgeries and exaggerations that they were long before Blair went to war. George Bush's references to the 'Niger' uranium connection with Iraq had been used even in his State of the Union address – long after the CIA realized that the 'evidence' was composed of forgeries. The so-called links between Iraq and al-Qa'ida could never be proved. Saddam was linked to the international crimes against humanity of 11 September 2001, Americans were told.

That one of the war's prime movers – the odd, dangerous Donald Rumsfeld, surrounded by his cabal of neo-conservative, pro-Israeli advisers – should have spent his time in 1983 cosying up to Saddam in order to re-open the US embassy in Baghdad, was ignored as an irrelevance. That Saddam had been 'our' tyrant for more than a decade was forgotten.

We were going to 'liberate' Iraq, just as the Crusaders had 'liberated' the Christians of the Middle East in the eleventh and twelfth centuries, just as Napoleon had 'liberated' Egypt in the eighteenth century, just as the British had 'liberated' Iraq and Palestine in the early twentieth. Saddam was a threat to us all.

But of course, he wasn't – only to his own, enslaved people. There were no weapons of mass destruction – they had long ago been abandoned. There was no 'imminent' threat of Iraqi attack on any of us. There were no al-Qa'ida links. There was no Iraqi connection to 11 September 2001. There was just oil and a broken country which we, the victors, allowed to become a symbol of anarchy.

Never before, perhaps, have governments of the 'free world' acted in such brazen opposition to the will of their own people – or conned them so thoroughly into believing the lies of their leaders. The damage done to Iraq was ultimately not so irremediable as the damage done to our own belief in popular democracy. Worse still, even after the fraudulent claims had been exposed, Messers Bush and Blair went on insisting that their lies represented the truth, that Iraq was a success story, that reality could be 'bent' in order to prove fantasy.

And this 'success' will become ever more illusory. Their map of the Middle East will turn out to have been changed forever, just as Bush, Rumsfeld and his sinister advisers claimed – but not in the way they predicted. The Middle East will be an ever more terrifying place for westerners, for Europeans and Americans alike, for Arabs – especially the Palestinians – and for the Israelis whose own self-proclaimed supporters helped to drive this insane war. Perhaps the Iraqis, who suffered so atrociously when we supported Saddam, will themselves help to destroy Bush and Blair. Many in Britain and America will be happy if they do. The United Nations, having been trashed as an international whore by Bush in the run-up to his illegal invasion, was in the end asked to save the lives of American soldiers by taking over the occupation.

In the meantime, one can only recall another British soldier of the 1914-18 war, who wrote of the British colonial administration in the very same way, words that we journalists have been using about America's post-war occupation. 'The Baghdad communiqués are belated, insincere, incomplete. Things are far worse than we have been told . . . We are today not far short of a disaster'. Lawrence of Arabia wrote this as the Iraqis started their brutal guerrilla war against British occupation in 1920. Would that we learned from history.

Beirut, 4 September 2003

Antonia Fraser

1. I was strongly against it. Tony Blair predicted confidently of this interventionist war: 'History will forgive us. . .' But History is not about predictions for the future – leave that to soothsayers and spin-doctors – it is about the study of the past, and trying if possible to learn something from it. More to the point, the philosopher George Santayana, a Spaniard educated at Harvard, wrote in 1905 in *The Life of Reason*: 'Those who cannot remember the past, are condemned to fulfil it.' The study of History in

advance would have shown Tony Blair and his government that Anglo-American co-operation at its most successful must include the possibility of holding back (as the infinitely cleverer, wilier Wilson managed to do in Vietnam) and never slavish adherence against the will of most of their countrymen. Even a quick look at the inception and development of the Vietnam War would have done more good than an awestruck trip to Bush Junior's Texas ranch.

2. Of course I hope that it will. One should always hope for lasting peace even if one is always disappointed. Apart from anything else, that way the relatives of those that have died, Iraqi, English and American, would have some kind of consolation. All I can say is that there is no sign of it yet.

17 September 2003

Jonathan Freedland

When Tony Blair goes to war, which is rather often, I usually find myself supporting him. I keenly backed the 1999 Nato operation in Kosovo, believing that it was not only in a just cause – the prevention of ethnic cleansing – but that it might even be the harbinger of a better, 21st century world to come: a world in which 'the international community' would no longer stand by and watch the commission of hideous crimes.

I reluctantly supported the 2001 offensive against Afghanistan. I supported it because I believe in the basic right of self-defence and the US had clearly been attacked on 11 September by a force based, however loosely, in that country. Reluctantly, because I did not believe, and still don't, that merely pounding a faraway country would come close to defeating al-Qa'ida, which is a much stranger, more diffuse kind of enemy.

So, by rights, I should have backed Tony Blair's mission in Iraq. After all, the result has been the toppling of a vile regime and the capture of its tyrannical leader. If the argument for Kosovo was that the world should no longer tolerate evil regimes, then who could object to Operation Iraqi Freedom?

I did, and do, because though 'moral interventionism' was indeed the basis of the Kosovo war, it was not the basis of this one. Admittedly, no sooner had Saddam's regime been toppled, with the tyrant himself captured eight months later, than London and Washington moved to pretend that this was what their war had been about all along. But it was not.

Tony Blair's case was that Iraq posed a direct threat to Britain and British interests because of its weapons of mass destruction. George W Bush added that Iraq harboured terrorists, had links to al-Qa'ida and, according to his Vice-President, may well have been behind the 9/11 attacks. These were the grounds on which the war was justified.

To my mind both were, at best, doubtful and, at worst, palpably false. There was no credible evidence to link Saddam with al-Qa'ida, still less with 9/11. And the evidence of an imminent threat from ready-to-fire Iraqi WMDs was flimsy. Former and current UN inspectors, along with those who had scrutinized Iraq throughout the 1990s, were just not convinced Saddam had the arsenal Bush and Blair said he had. I also believed, along with former President Clinton, that an adventure in Iraq would distract from fighting the real enemy, which remained al-Qa'ida.

Isn't all this a bit purist, not to say prissy? If Bush and Blair's war was always going to achieve a noble outcome, Saddam's removal, then isn't it a touch pedantic to oppose that war just because it was fought for the wrong reasons? I don't think so. Sending young men and women to kill and be killed is a serious business. The governments of great nations cannot do it on a false prospectus; they cannot do it on the basis of a double lie. For if we let them, they will do it again.

18 December 2003

Nadine Gordimer

I was totally against the American war on Iraq, and I deplore the almost general *laissez faire* attitude of the world to the obvious power-manipulations evidenced in the bungled and bloody 'reconstruction' of the country . . . It was clear from the beginning that the invasion would result in a situation amounting close to civil war, the scenario for that readied in the wings of the scene by history. The consistent factor in all present conflicts is the vast gap between rich and poor, and the subliminal racism that continues, under the seven veils of democracy, to justify it.

21 June 2003

David Guterson

I deplore the American-led military action against Saddam Hussein's regime in March and April of 2003. If the American government's express purpose is national and global security, it seems patently clear to me that these aims can not be achieved through unilateral aggression. America will only have peace and security when it sincerely addresses the legitimate grievances arrayed against it around the world. Will this happen? I'm highly doubtful. The blind greed of American capitalism, its inherent immorality, means many more centuries of horrendous suffering, much of it perpetuated by America in the Orwellian name of peace and freedom.

19 June 2003

David Hare

I was taken aback by the lying. George Bush lied when he pretended Iraq represented a threat to the United States. He lied, saying it was a current or increased threat to its neighbours. He lied when he pretended it possessed nuclear weapons. He lied shamelessly when he sought to relate Iraq to al-Qa'ida and 11 September, with which it had no connection. And finally, as I write, he may be found to have lied when he said it still had chemical weapons of mass destruction. Beyond the mendacity, Bush sought deliberately to work outside the authority of the United Nations, and to blacken the name of its weapons inspectors and other members of the Security Council, who were, in retrospect and at the time, right about everything. The pre-emptive attack had nothing to pre-empt, so it was doubly wrong in principle. It was also hideous in execution.

Will an illegal invasion bring peace? Has one, ever?

4 June 2003

Adam Hart-Davis

Unless it or one of its allies is attacked, no country should ever invade another. Neither the United States, nor the United Kingdom, nor any of their allies, was attacked by Iraq. Saddam Hussein was a tyrant, but the reasons we were given for the Anglo-American invasion of Iraq in 2003 were specious.

As for the aftermath, there is no sign that this invasion has brought peace or stability to the Middle East.

2 June 2003

John Heath-Stubbs

I was for the war, though with some reservations. In fact I am inclined to think it should have followed from the first Gulf War. Although WMD have not been found, Saddam's previous actions made it likely that he would have them.

There is no guarantee that the intervention will bring lasting peace.

3 July 2003

Bevis Hillier

When I was asked to contribute to *Authors Take Sides on the Falklands* in 1982, I was able to give a clear answer to the question: was the Thatcher government right to engage in conflict with Argentina in that year? Argentina had invaded what was, in international law as it then stood, our territory; the Argentinians had been given ample opportunity to get out; and the inhabitants of the Falklands *wanted* them out.

I remember feeling proud that Mary Renault – with her great historical sense – gave a similar unequivocal 'yes' in the same book. I am not a devilish imperialist, as the renegade Etonian Neal Ascherson implied in a review. It did seem to make rather more sense that the Falklands ('Malvinas') should be part of nearby Argentina than part of the possessions of an island thousands of miles away; but illegal invasion was not the way to resolve the dispute, and of course the wishes of the Falkland Islanders had to be taken into account.

I was much less sure that Britain was right to join military action against Saddam Hussein in 2003. He had not invaded our territory. No convincing evidence was produced that he was in league with bin Laden – though he may have been. I knew he was a foul dictator, and that Iraq and the world would be better off without him – but both America and Britain were denying that 'regime change' was their object.

The old appeasers' argument comes into play: are we to tilt against every filthy dictator in the world? Our work will be cut out. Zimbabwe? Iran? China? Is little Britain to be the policeman of the world? That argument always sounds to me a bit like, 'I'm not giving anything to a beggar in the Strand because there are so many in India – it's a drop in the ocean.' ('Every little helps,' as the duchess said when she peed in the Atlantic.) Or again, in reverse, it is like the blissful selfishness of those who maintain that, because they were lucky enough to have been born on a pleasant plot of land (Great

Britain) they are not going to forfeit one atom of their comfort to help, say, people escaping from flood-devastated Bangladesh, or genuine asylum-seekers.

It is suggested that we took action against Saddam without proper United Nations sanction. To that I would reply that, first, the UN is a structurally corrupt organization, in which liaisons between countries are formed for reasons other than the desire to achieve strict international justice; second, France will always cravenly opt out, as she did in World War II; and third, what Kofi Annan was requesting, in his polite, conciliatory way, was more time for the weapons inspectors to do their job. That would have meant more time for Saddam to torture and murder thousands more Iraqi citizens; and weather conditions would have become progressively less favourable for our armed forces – imperilling American and British lives. Besides, if Saddam had no WMDs, none would be found; if he did have them, no doubt the cunning bastard would find means of hiding them (as the American and British governments are busy claiming now – 7 June 2003 – he has done).

Historians speak of kings *de jure* and *de facto*. Either sort may turn out good or ghastly. Our victory – won in a miraculously short time, and with comparatively few allied casualties – may be more *de facto* than *de jure*; but it has rid Iraq of a monstrous tyranny – I imagine that even the Aschersons of this world will concede that.

Your second question: 'Do you believe that the intervention will bring about lasting peace and stability in the region?' An unfortunate start has been made. Because (I suspect) the Americans and British foresaw tougher opposition and a longer conflict, they made inadequate provision for the peace: hence the initial looting and general anarchy. I am not sure whether your question refers to Iraq in particular, or to the Middle East in general, but in either case – just as in Ireland – the baleful influence of warring religions is felt. Where religion takes precedence in the minds of people, political sanctions are impotent: look at Louis XIV and the Camisards of the Cevennes.

But let me be more optimistic. In *The Garden of Proserpine* Swinburne wrote:

Even the weariest river
Winds somewhere safe to sea.

Evil regimes never last forever: to a degree, they die from their own poison. Nazism bit the dust. Soviet Communism was defeated – and may I point out to Mr Ascherson, that was partly through our *having* nuclear weapons to match the Soviets'. I admit nuclear weapons are a terrible worry, and I trembled in the Cuba crisis of 1962. But 'Ban the bomb' was always a delusory parrot-cry: once the A-bomb and the H-bomb were invented, the lid was off Pandora's Box and there was no putting it back again. Which side would ever have believed that the other had in fact 'banned the bomb'? Which side would ever have relinquished its bombs?

It is by strength, not feebleness, that evil is defeated. The allied victory in Iraq is a good illustration of that rather obvious theorem. My old friend Simon Jenkins – the appeasers' appeaser – often savagely and satirically quotes the words, 'We will bomb our way to the conference table'. I'm afraid there is sometimes no other way.

7 June 2003

Richard Hoggart

1.Unwillingly, yes; because of Saddam Hussein's long record; and on the (now doubtful understanding that he was collecting more WMDs.
2. Not lasting peace. But it might delay and deter for a while.

10 July 2003

Michael Holroyd

I was against the American-led invasion of Iraq. I thought the reasons given for it were inadequate and the evidence presented in support of them largely fabricated. Iraq has no nuclear weapons (which are the only real 'weapons of mass destruction') and did not threaten New York or London. Did you feel threatened? Nor did I: but I feel more vulnerable now since we must obviously and understandably be prime targets for violent retaliation. That would be acceptable perhaps if the ethical justification for war was overwhelming. But it never was. When I listened to Kofi Annan or Robin Cook, I heard the sound of truth. When I saw Donald Rumsfeld and George W Bush on television, I was reminded of those ambitious businessmen who rose to power after the disgraceful Versailles Treaty. And when Jack Straw stood up to speak, dressed in his brief authority, some lines from *King Lear* came back to me: 'Get thee glass eyes; / And, like a scurvy politician, seem / To see things thou dost not'. But what of Tony Blair? He was as sincere as believers in the Flat Earth were sincere. He was sincerely wrong, sincerely self-deceived, sincerely praying to love one's enemies and turn the other cheek on a Sunday, and sincerely going to war on a Monday. In short, he was, with deep sincerity, drawn to the magnet of power: the United States. I believe that history will show him to have been a sincerely dangerous man.

12 May 2003

Michael Horovitz

My friend the poet Harry Eyres has translated lines 505 to 511 of Virgil's *Georgics* as follows:

> . . . Round here it's upside-down; atrocity
> Instead of righteousness; so many wars
> Spread all over earth, so multiple
> The faces of wrong-doing; the peaceful plough
> Abandoned, farmers violently evicted,
> The untended fields despoiled to waste land,
> Curved pruning hooks, estranged from vines,
> Battered into the rigidness of swords
>
> . . . and neighbouring
> Cities scrap their peace accords and fight
> And the murderous war-god ravens everywhere.

Virgil wrote the *Georgics* thirty years before the birth of Christ. Two thousand years and hundreds of pointless wars later Bob Dylan, among millions of others, sang it again:

> . . . While money doesn't talk, it swears
> Obscenity, who really cares
> Propaganda, all is phony.

The American-led military action against Saddam was bound, by definition, to reinforce the philosophy and effects of international terrorism and of Saddam's regime – i.e., that brute force is the ultimate god and defining arbiter of politics in our time.

Evil dictators thrive and weapons of mass destruction proliferate all over the planet, and many nations cosied up to by Britain and the US are in breach of many United Nations resolutions.

Britain and the US have long encouraged (and continue even now to encourage) these nations to manufacture, buy and sell all manner of weapons, including massively destructive ones. Tax payers have long subsidized this death trade, and even now are constrained to continue to do so.

Military intervention has not brought either peace or stability to Afghanistan, and seems at least as unlikely to bring them to Iraq. Warlords breed warlords and terror breeds terror, and every violent act extends the uncontrollable power of the murderous war-god.

Bush and Blair prate of moral priorities – but what have they done? Their coalition has invested over two hundred billion dollars in the Iraq war, but scarcely one billion to combat the spread of Aids across Africa (that far-off continent dubbed by Blair 'a scar upon the conscience of the world'). How moral is that?

And yet these prime movers of this sorry saga, daily continuing to detonate the injury and killing of thousands of blameless human beings, continue to invoke 'humanitarian aid', 'civilized values' and the teachings of Jesus Christ, as the guiding lights of their knee-jerk war-mongering. To most objective observers – let alone to their diverse victims – Presidents Bash and Blur, secretaries Rumsfeld and Straw, and their brain-zapped armies of henchfolk, look and sound more like Tweedledum and Tweedledee than upholders of any sacred flame.

Let them pause, before thousands more lives are threatened to no palpable purpose, and take a few basic questions seriously. Such as:

Is not a reverence
for life – for all land, sea and air
the path Jesus struck,
Shock and Awe Basher Bush,
Trade and War Preacher Blair?

Have you no shame?

How can you claim
to follow Christ,
when your fame has spread
so many dark days and nights
with more dead
across so many lands, from your hands
—famed oily blood brothers
who wreak so much hurt, loss and fright
—dread of so many children and mothers
with your gospel of markets and self-righteous might

whose weapons ignite still more terror and plight,
filling land, sea and air
with endless infection, bombs and despair?

'Love thy neighbour
as thyself',
NOT
'An eye for an eye',
is what Jesus preached,
Big Top Barker Bush,
And your yapping
Dog-collared Upsucking
Mascot Blair.

4 October 2003

Christine Jordis

This war was both a crime and a mistake, as was the Iraq war of 1991. This war was illegal, and it is not the fact that part of its consequences – the fall of Saddam Hussein – is a positive event, that makes it legal.

Let me first point out that the Bush government undertook the operation without the consent of the UN and under false pretences, as they now have to recognize, even if Mr Tony Blair doesn't. It now appears that there was no threat of nuclear weapons, no threat at all. As for the war against terrorism, it is a very convenient and vague pretext which should apply equally to the French or English suburbs, where potential terrorists are also agitating. Why not? Why shouldn't the US attack these suburbs, since force seems to be the only response to terrorism? The law of the gun, as in the good, old days.

There was no justification for the United States to invade Iraq, except to spread their liberal order throughout the world with the intention of dominating it. Economic and strategic reasons – oil – were part of the equation.

They ignored international law, trampled on world opinion, used brute force to serve their own interests and their will to hegemony. They attacked and destroyed a country which they had already bombarded for a decade, leaving uranium and radioactive waste. Through a protracted blockade, this country had already been deprived of many of the necessities of survival, weakened to an extreme point, and thousands of children had died. How can anyone speak of a 'victory'? If there is any victory, it is one of shame.

The US wiped out half a century of human conquests in the field of international rights. As to the values that they brandish and use as a screen – good *versus* evil, freedom, liberation: they merely demonstrate their capacity to distort the language and the meaning of words, exactly as the rulers of the Soviet Union did. Words have no more sense, or only that which a dominant force imposes through the use of bombs and weapons.

As for the people who sincerely supported the war, 'the deluded idiots', as Harold Pinter said of T. Blair – their position is an indication of the widespread arrogance in the West, the belief that ours are superior values and we have a right to impose them on the world, without for a moment considering whether the world is willing or ready to adopt them. The role of self-appointed sheriff is an unacceptable one.

This leads us to the second question. To intervene in a region like the Middle East requires intensive study, not only of the targeted country, but also of the subtle interrelations between the neighbouring countries. The Bush government has signally failed to do that, As a result, chaos follows war, more bombing, more killing, nothing approximating to peace. And growing hatred. What we have is a bloody, interminable, costly pacification.

This was the case in Afghanistan, where we see nothing like democracy emerging; it is now the case in Iraq. Let us not talk of the fact that the US first armed the Taliban, only to wage war against them later. The same pattern emerges in Iraq, but even worse, where they could have changed the regime after the 1991 war, but decided not to, for reasons of political and economic expediency.

To import a ready-made US democracy into the Middle East is a chimera. We see rebellion, fighting and great unhappiness: in short, a state that seems to be just as bad as under Saddam Hussein, but perhaps less acceptable and more humiliating to the native population.

The results of the negotiations in Israel, if they are successful, might help the US to recover some credibility.

16 June 2003

H.R.F. Keating

A novelist, I think, tends to view the world from a slightly skewed angle. Events, to my eyes, are reflections of the characters of the people who cause them to happen. So, how did I see Tony Blair? As a human being, and therefore flawed. As a young man full of enthusiasm, as he certainly was when he first came to power amid general rejoicing. On that day I was on a bus in London when the conductor strode to the front end, raised both his ar ms wide, and called out 'This is a great day'. I felt it so. And, years later, I felt something of the same enthusiasm when a slightly older Tony Blair, on 12 September 2001, flung himself and the nation with him to stand beside the bereaved people of New York and all America. Alas, in March 2003, when I had watched President Bush on television belabouring Iraq, I felt I could no longer go along with Tony Blair, though I gave him credit for his loyalty to a long-ago cause.

And the novelist's view of George Bush? It is hard to delve behind the outward shape of the bully boy. Yes, he loves his dogs. So there must be affection there. But, no, the spectacle of the Texan gun-fighter, thinking of almost nothing but the kill, must mean that one who tries to see all sides of any person who comes to their notice, can only feel that President Bush is as dangerous a man as Saddam Hussein. And that Britain, in so far as it was possible, should not have embarked on the Bush crusade.

13 July 2003

John Keegan

I was and am strongly for the military action taken against the Saddam Hussein regime in Iraq in March and April 2003, as I was for the war to expel his forces from Kuwait in 1991. I was also, with reservations, a supporter of the British government's decision to recover the Falklands in 1982 and the American intervention in Vietnam. Kingsley Amis summarized admirably the reasons I had for supporting American fighting in Vietnam.

It is impossible to say what effect the intervention will have in the region, where neither peace nor stability has prevailed since the high days of the Ottoman Empire. In general I am pessimistic about the future of the historic Muslim lands – Syria, Saudi Arabia, Iraq, Iran and Algeria (though not Morocco or Egypt) – for reasons which have to do with the late mediaeval decision in Islam to renounce the pursuit of progress. I except Egypt because of its persisting tradition of non-Islamic nationalism and Morocco because of the strength of its monarchical institutions.

In general, I believe that the use of force, by states and armies that embody civilized values, can achieve good. I have no sympathy with those who shrink from the use of force as if it were in itself a bad thing. Such people seem to me the disease to the cure.

2 June 2003

Thomas Keneally

I was dead against the military action against Saddam Hussein 's regime. I thought it gratuitous and likely to create more terrorists in the West and also to be an intervention which did *not* bring lasting peace but which exposed all the conflicts within Iraq and which would commit the Allies to a virtually endless police action, which is now happening.

And I don't know how a dumbcluck in Australia, who knew about the divisions between Shias and the Sunni, could work that out while the State Department in Washington couldn't. It is a breathtaking act of irresponsibility on the part of at least three governments, the British, the Americans and the Australian.

18 September 2003

Francis King

During the last war I became a pacifist land-worker. But as the war progressed and more and more acts of Nazi barbarism came to light, I began increasingly to wonder whether my youthfully idealistic decision had been the right one. I still wonder. It is impossible to balance what actually occurred against what might have occurred and so to arrive at a comparison between an actual sum of suffering and a hypothetical one. On the one side of the scales there is the terrible reality of the millions killed and maimed, historic cities ravaged or totally destroyed, the obliteration of works of arts of incalculable value, the Soviet domination of Eastern Europe, the Gulag, and the atom bomb. On the other side, if there had been no resistance to the Germans, there is – what? We can only guess.

I waver similarly over the recent war (I hate the euphemism 'military action') in Iraq. No one could have been unmoved by those pictures of mutilated children and grieving adults, or of the chaos of cities deprived of all public services and subjected to mindless looting. But what would have been the sum of suffering if the coalition had never taken action? Again one can only guess. Saddam Hussein's regime was a monstrous one, which killed many more people over a period of years than the coalition did in a few weeks. The Marsh Arabs alone, subjected to a campaign of unrelenting genocide, died in far greater numbers. It seems certain that the barbarity and corruption would have continued.

In the end, my conclusion is that this was a righteous war but one started for the wrong reason. Repeated acts of genocide and the shameless violation of human rights, not the possible continuing existence of weapons of mass destruction, constitute the justification that works for me.

The most that I now hope for is that there will be an emergence of some form of democracy in Iraq, and that Iraq's neighbours, frightened by the example of the nemesis that engulfed a state so close to them, may gradually retreat from their own despotic and intolerant forms of government.

The region is far too volatile and the Israeli-Arab conflict far too long-standing and bitter for me to have any expectation of a lasting peace.

12 May 2003

John le Carré

I opposed the war before it began, wrote against it in *The Times* and marched against it in London. I believed then, and believe now, that this illegal and unprovoked invasion will lead to greater instability and suffering in the region than existed before it was launched.

But we should not overlook the damage it has done to us, and to our leaders: the damage to our reputation in the world, and to our self-respect. The lies and falsifications concocted by the two main aggressors and cravenly echoed by the appallingly docile American and British media will reverberate to our disgrace for generations to come. We in the West will of course quickly forget. The victims never will.

11 June 2003

Robert Littell

Impossible not to celebrate the fall of Saddam Hussein and the liberation of twenty-three million people from his brutal dictatorship. Having said that, I must add that it is impossible, too, not to have serious misgivings about the administration's justification for intervention (the new and improved doctrine of 'pre-emption') as well as Bush's ability to manage the end game in such a way that a unified and dignified Iraq emerges from the chaos of pre-emption. On top of that, it is impossible not to wince at the way the Republicans are using the so-called war against terrorism, and the so-called victory in Iraq, to shamelessly advance a neo-conservative agenda designed to starve the government of money and under-fund or kill domestic social programs – this despite the fact that Bush campaigned as a 'compassionate conservative'. No wonder right-thinking people are left with the impression that Bush & Company (who lost the presidential election by half a million votes) have hijacked the American government. Having liberated Iraq, we must now liberate America!

31 May 2003

David Lodge

On 2 April 2003, about two weeks into the war, I published an article on the subject commissioned by the Swiss newspaper *Neue Zürcher Zeitung*. I wrote:

I have a bad feeling about this war. I think Saddam Hussein is an evil monster and I would rejoice to see him removed from power; but I don't think our soldiers should be in that country, killing its citizens and risking their own lives, in order to achieve that end . . . Saddam is not a serious enough threat to our safety to justify, either legally or morally, a pre-emptive invasion of Iraq; we cannot be certain of keeping civilian casualties within acceptable limits; even if victory is achieved the consequences of the war for the Iraqi people are unpredictable and may well make a bad situation worse; the war can only have the effect of inflaming Arab opinion against us and encouraging Islamist terrorism.

I still take this position, but I did not find it easy to reach, and I have not found it easy to hold to subsequently. I differ from those of my fellow-countrymen, on both the Left and the Right, who believe that whether to support or oppose the war was a simple issue, and who are 100% convinced of the rightness of their own opinion. Once this exceptionally arrogant, intransigent and imperialistic American administration had made up its mind to go to war, Britain was faced with the uncomfortable choice of either opposing the policy but not affecting the eventual outcome, or supporting it in the hope of exerting some control over it, and its sequels. I don't condemn Tony Blair unreservedly for taking the second course. It is increasingly clear that Saddam Hussein's regime was an exceptionally evil one, and very unlikely that it would have fallen without armed intervention from outside. But in the end the question of legality still tips the balance for me. The ostensible justification of the war – to remove the threat of weapons of mass destruction – was always unconvincing and seems increasingly so as (at the time of writing this) they fail to materialize. Invading a sovereign country without satisfying the normal criteria of a 'just war' sets a very dangerous precedent in the post-cold-war era, and is unlikely to produce lasting peace and stability in the Middle East or the world. But we won't know for years whether the war did more harm than good, or vice versa.

8 June 2003

Richard Mayne

I forget who said of quarrelling neighbours: 'They'll find it hard to agree: they're arguing from different premises.' That certainly applies to Europe and America over Iraq. Each still misreads the other. Some on either side still misread militant Islam.

Many Europeans underestimate the trauma that 9/11 caused their American friends. In World War II, most European countries suffered enemy bombing and, at one stage or another, occupation. Even Britain, spared invasion save for the Channel Islands, grew accustomed to the nightly blitz. The United States had no such experience. There were invasion scares, and fear of Japanese infiltration; but the homeland —evocative term – remained inviolate. If wars, for the British, were something they fought in other countries, they were even more so for the Americans. World War II was an away game – 'over there', as they sang in World War I. 9/11 brought tragedy home.

Not that Americans had escaped slaughter. A second aspect of the American psyche that Europeans may underplay is awareness of how many American lives have been lost fighting Europe's battles for it. If the United States has become a world policeman, it has done so reluctantly, and at great cost. No wonder that Americans resent reproaches from Europeans who, even now, spends much less on security and defence. To patriotic Americans, some European statesmen seem ungrateful, oblivious of the debt they owe to the American dead.

A third fact that Europeans may forget is America's experience in Vietnam. Famously the first televized war, it showed to civilians some of war's reality, and spawned a horror of body bags. Despite superior US hardware, it was the first war America had lost. And although it began with high intentions, to stem a supposed 'domino topple' into Communism, for many Americans it was the first conflict in which they feared their soldiers were not fighting for a just cause.

But if Europeans misread America, Americans misread Europe. Some have little idea of how the Bush administration looks to many people in the old world – or 'Old Europe', in Donald Rumsfeld's dismissive phrase.

It began with George W Bush's election. Forgetting the anomalies of their own electoral systems, some Europeans see the electoral college as having thwarted a democratic (and Democrat) majority of the voters, and the disputed Florida vote, with its 'hanging chads' and suspicions of rigging, as having handed the decision to a single conservative judge in the Supreme Court.

The administration's composition, rhetoric, and behaviour are further sore points. Rightly or wrongly, Europeans have accused some of its members of unduly close links with oil. They have demurred from its neo-conservative, born-again, fundamentalist language. And they have deplored some of its policies quite apart from Iraq, — beef hormones, GM foodstuffs, and the now resolved but not unique tariff on steel.

Iraq, however, is the sorest point of all. Not many Europeans have or had any time for Saddam Hussein. Most are glad his régime is gone. A few, with *realpolitisch* disregard of law and the United Nations, even wished that George Bush senior had pressed on to Baghdad. But many question whether pre-emptive action was necessary or wise, and whether 'shock and awe' will ever win hearts and minds. They said then, and think now, that although there was no clear link between Saddam and al-Qa'ida, the Iraq war has created one in retrospect, giving the terrorists a further pretext for violence. Some also wonder whether a democratic Iraq, if it can be achieved, may not turn out to be theocratic – or prone to civil war.

The last – and most lasting – bone of contention is Israel. This is not, as some claim, the only issue fuelling al-Qa'ida's fury. America periodically seems to lose patience with Ariel Sharon, and George W Bush has backed the call for Palestinian statehood. But is the pro-Israeli vote in the United States a sufficient argument for America's not seconding repeated European calls for Israeli withdrawal to legal borders – not to mention the dismantling of the infamous fence or wall?

Looking back, however, is useful only if it reveals deep-seated attitudes that need future attention, and illuminates errors we should not repeat. As with the countryman asked the way and saying he wouldn't start from here, regretting the past is pointless. What lessons can we learn?

For Europeans and Americans, the first answer might be: Arabic – or, at least, more about Islam. Humiliation can be tragically explosive. Germany was humiliated at Versailles: the result was National Socialism. Much of continental Europe was humiliated in World War II, but saved by statesmen from many countries. Harry S. Truman and George Marshall helped to regain prosperity. Jean Monnet, Robert Schuman, Konrad Adenauer, Alcide de Gasperi, and Paul-Henri Spaak helped it unite to recover self-respect and influence. Humiliated in some degree by Vietnam, America was outraged by 9/11, and reacted with brute force.

Islam has suffered in similar ways. A great civilizing force, whose philosophers rescued Greek thought for mediaeval Europe and taught the West mathematics and much else, it has found itself opposed by 'Crusaders', then outpaced by technology, and ignored or spurned by materialists with no firm belief in an after-life. Fundamentalist Muslims, convinced that the world's rich countries are on the wrong path, find it easy to recruit the poor, ignorant and fanatical into a new *jihad* that in modern terms mirrors the Crusades.

Europeans and Americans need to understand and engage with representatives of Islam who respect and follow the basically peaceful, tolerant precepts of the Koran. Is dialogue possible with the others? Perhaps, if conducted by their co-religionists – though relations between Sunnis and Shias in Iraq are hardly encouraging. What is certain is that 'shock and awe' are not enough.

How, then, should we Europeans seek to influence matters? Clearly, by influencing the United States. Some Europeans, for a time, tried blunt opposition. It was not a success. Britain, notably, tried co-operation and broad compliance. That led us to where we are now.

The real answer, surely, is that single European countries carry too little weight. Only together, and only by making far bigger efforts to match United States defence and security efforts, can the European Union rebuild what J.F. Kennedy acknowledged and worked for – neither subservience nor hostility, but a transatlantic partnership of equals.

6 December 2003

Michael Morpurgo

To me there can be only one sound, valid, moral reason for going to war, for fighting: self-defence. We all knew we were not threatened in any way by Iraq. This was a contrived war, invented to further a right-wing agenda in the US. We simply went along meekly clinging to Uncle Sam's coat-tails. It was and is wicked, cruel and morally indefensible. I felt and feel deeply ashamed, sickened by the whole episode!

1 June 2003

Nicholas Mosley

I was against the war in Iraq because the American and British governments produced no evidence to substantiate their stated reasons for going to war. It thus appeared that either they were liars, or their intelligence services were half-witted.

It seems to me inconceivable that lasting peace and stability will come to the area. On the other hand there is evidence that fundamentalist terrorism has to be fought, and so some good may come out of acts of savage arrogance.

2 June 2003

Andrew Motion

I was against the war in Iraq, and do not feel confident that it will bring about lasting peace and stability in the region. The enclosed poem, which appeared in the *Guardian* and elsewhere, is the best answer I can give,

Regime Change

Advancing down the road from Niniveh
Death paused a while and said 'Now listen here.

You see the names of places roundabout?
They're mine now, and I've turned them inside out.

Take Eden, further south: at dawn today
I ordered up my troops to tear away

its walls and gates so everyone can see
that gorgeous fruit which dangles from its tree.

Take Tigris and Euphrates; once they ran
through childhood-coloured slats of sand and sun.

Not any more they don't; I've filled them up
with countless different kinds of human crap.

Take Babylon, the palace sprouting flowers

which sweetened empires in their peaceful hours –

I've found a different way to scent the air:
already it's a by-word for despair.

Which leaves Baghdad — the star-tipped minarets,
the marble courts and halls, the mirage-heat.

These places, and the ancient things you know,
you won't know soon. I'm working on it now.'

7 May 2003

Ferdinand Mount

I started life as an apprehensive dove. Over the years I have become a tentative hawk. At the time I regarded the Falklands operation as a quixotic venture and in my heart wondered how necessary it was. Since then I have gradually become convinced that the calibrated use of force to get rid of mass murderers may sometimes be justified by the consequences. Retaking the Falklands destroyed Galtieri and dictatorship in Argentina and may have helped to spread democracy through South America. Even so I was sympathetic to the Western reluctance to intervene in Bosnia and Kosovo until after thousands of Muslims had been murdered, and sympathetic too in the first Gulf War to the coalition's decision to abide by the letter of the UN resolution and not to press on to Baghdad. Twelve years on, after the pile of Saddam's victims had mounted even higher, I was and am firmly convinced of the case for pre-emptive action (if you can call waiting for twelve years pre-emptive).

There was always a risk of the coalition looking foolish if they failed to find substantial stocks of Weapons of Mass Destruction *in situ*, but the greatest WMDs were Saddam and his sons and I rejoice in their departure from the scene as fervently as I mourn the dead on both sides.

Terrorism is likely to continue in the Middle East and elsewhere for many years to come, and it is far too early to predict that the war will produce 'lasting peace and stability in the region', but I am convinced that the ramshackle democracies which are likely to spread, though at a slower pace than they did in South America, will be infinitely preferable to the corrupt, bloodstained and aggressive dictatorships which for so long have squashed hopes of progress in the Arab world.

This war and to a lesser extent the Afghanistan conflict which closely preceded it have also changed the terms of the moral argument. War launched by a great power (at present the only great power) against a much weaker opponent has lost at least one of its old horrors, that of unpredictable escalation and unknowable human cost. Proportionality – that desirable concept to which men of goodwill have subscribed since Thomas Aquinas – comes closer to practical reality. In Iraq, despite all the gloomy predictions, the United States was in fact able to pinpoint military targets with far fewer civilian casualties than in any of the great bombardments of the twentieth century and also to forecast with reasonable accuracy the likely length and cost of hostilities.

This is certainly no excuse for the Americans to lapse into trigger-happy triumphalism. War is still ghastly. But in a limited number of cases it does mean that going in becomes a legitimate moral option which has to be carefully measured against staying out. Growing older does at least allow you to observe the cumulative costs of doing nothing.

20 May 2003

Thomas Nydahl

Let me first of all say, I am not against all forms of military action. I think that post-war Europe from 1945 would have been a great Nazi empire had military action against the German Reich not been taken. I think the tragedies in Bosnia, Croatia and Kosovo would have been even worse had not the outside world been involved to stop the bloodshed and ethnic cleansing.

But I was against the military action against Iraq, because I think the key issue in the Middle East is the Palestinian problem. As long as the Palestinian people live in poverty and humiliation under occupation, there is no way forward. My suspicion that the American-led invasion was motivated by oil and the wealth of the Iraqi nation was confirmed some weeks ago by senior American officials: 'to disarm Saddam was just a diplomatic formula that everyone could accept'. Where are the weapons of mass destruction? Why was there not a single Iraqi fighter in the air during the war, why no chemical or biological missiles launched against Israel, Saudi Arabia or the coalition forces?

Today I watched the news bulletin about continuing military clashes in Iraq – more than 100 people killed in one day. The same day we hear of demonstrations in Iran against the Mullahs, suicide bombers in Jerusalem and heavy Israeli helicopter attacks in the Gaza strip. The al-Qa'ida network is active all over the world. A man in Bangkok was arrested with 35 kg of highly radioactive cesium. So much in today's world of the 'war against terrorism' is interconnected. The Iraq problem can not be solved by occupation, any more than the suffering Afghan nation is going to achieve peace and prosperity through the presence of 'the international community'. No occupation is history tells us anything else. Sooner or later the occupying forces will have to leave, as they did in Algeria, in Vietnam, in Cambodia, in Afghanistan under Soviet rule, as in Eastern Europe after the fall of the Berlin wall, as in Africa or Asia, where the British, Portuguese and Spanish all had to leave. In the same way, the coalition will have to withdraw from Iraq. But that does not mean that peace and stability comes to the region. Perhaps it never will, because of the involvement of the hypocritical leaders of the great religions —Islam, Judaism and Christianity – and the wealth of the oil resources.

15 June 2003

Robert Nye

Taking 'sides' does not seem right in the circumstances, but I suppose I was for the Coalition action against Saddam Hussein's regime, even if reluctantly. I detest bloodshed, but it was good to see that statue coming down.

As to whether the intervention will bring about lasting peace and stability in the region: I don't believe it will, but I can hope it might.

8 May 2003

Six months on, such hope becomes harder to maintain.

3 December 2003

Peter Oborne

The attack on Iraq was driven by a disastrous conceptual error arising out of 11 September. President Bush and Tony Blair wanted to believe that terrorism was a conventional enemy. They therefore acted as if Iraq was somehow the headquarters of al-Qa'ida, just as the old USSR was the stronghold of Soviet Communism. In fact there was no link between international terrorism and Saddam Hussein.

The conceptual error means that the United States has done nothing to address the real grievances that underlay the 11 September attack. The use of military force to conquer surrogate targets does nothing to eradicate terrorism. All it achieves is the alienation of Muslim opinion and creation of the conditions for the emergence of a new generation of terrorists.

The struggle against al-Qa'ida will be long and horrible. So far we have set about the struggle in exactly the wrong way. By invading Iraq Britain and America have handed bin Laden a priceless propaganda gift. Britain performed the same sort of service for the IRA when troops shot dead 13 civil rights marchers at Derry on 30 January 1972. We paid the price for decades afterwards.

5 July 2003

Charles Osborne

With the benefit of hindsight, I am firmly against the American-led military attack on Iraq. At the time it happened, I understood why America thought it was avenging a ghastly assault on New York's Twin Towers, but it soon became evident that America's action was against Saddam Hussein and his regime. An evil regime, yes, but are his opponents in Iraq any better? In the name of religion, various sects violently, indeed murderously, oppose one another. It was ever thus in that part of the world, and no doubt it always will be. I'd be delighted to hear that Saddam Hussein and Osama bin Laden had been assassinated, but they would then be replaced by other terrorists (— or freedom-fighters, depending on one's point of view).

There will never be lasting peace or stability in the Muslim world. But can Christian countries consider themselves superior, while Protestants and Catholics still fight it out in Northern Ireland? A plague on all religion, say I.

15 September 2003

Sara Paretsky

I was against the American-led military action in Iraq. I did all in my power as a citizen to oppose this action, including writing and calling Congress and the President, submitting letters to the editor, marching and giving money to the effort. I believed, and still do believe, that, however despicable Saddam Hussein was, nothing warranted our attack on the country. On the contrary, I believed this was wrong in setting a precedent for any other country wanting to dislodge another country's government. I also believed this action would seriously destabilize the Middle East and would prove – as in fact it has proven – a fertile recruiting ground for terrorists.

31 October 2003

Melanie Phillips

I supported the war against Saddam. I also think that the groundswell of feeling against it in Britain is a symptom of a decadent culture that is not only unwilling to defend itself but is no longer susceptible to reason, logic and common-sense. Most of the arguments against the war were specious. This was no colonial adventure by a Texan cowboy, but a belated recognition of the magnitude of the threat to the West and the terrifying inadequacy of its response. Saddam had been developing his weapons of mass destruction while engaging in terrorist acts – including against the US – for years. America had gone along with the western consensus that terrorism should be appeased, until 9/11 changed its entire perspective and tore up the old *realpolitik*. Whether or not Saddam had been involved in 9/11 was irrelevant. What America suddenly realised was that terrorists backed by rogue states had declared war on the West and were intent on carrying it out. The risk that they might become equipped with chemical, biological or nuclear weapons was therefore no longer one that could be put on the back burner while the United Nations spun out the farce of negotiation. The war against Saddam was rational, moral and legal. He had been considered such a threat, even after he was removed from Kuwait in 1991, that it was made a cease-fire condition that he dismantle his WMD and prove he had done so. He refused for 12 years, during which time he sponsored terror while the weapons inspectors attested he was continuing to build up his WMD programme and that there were significant amounts of WMD unaccounted for. Only a fool would think that, despite all this, Saddam was less dangerous to the West in 2003 than he had been in 1991. The fault lay not in eventually going to war to enforce the UN's will, but with the UN for having given a strong signal for so many years that those who threatened the security of the world would be able to get away with it.

I think the US made some serious errors in the way it approached post-war Iraq. Rebuilding a stable and free society there was never going to be easy. And the wider war on terror is obviously fraught with danger. But I believe we have no real choice but to fight it. The West did not declare war on anyone; war has been declared on the West. That war is backed by a number of terror-sponsoring states, each of which has to have its fangs drawn. A free and stable Iraq would be a powerful destabilising force on those terror regimes. That is precisely why they have helped foment terrorism and unrest within Iraq. One cannot predict the outcome of all this; the attempt to face down terror is bound to be a long, difficult process with many setbacks. Peace and stability are still a long way off. But I believe the greatest single impulse behind the growth of world terror has been the understanding by rogue states that the West would never fight them but always seek to buy them off in some way. That is why I think America's abrupt change of approach – however flawed it may be in its detail – is critical to the eventual peace and security of the world, which is now threatened not just by global terror but, more insidiously, by the blinkered, feeble or positively malign culture of appeasement which opposes it.

25 September 2003

Ben Pimlott

You'd have to be mad not to be on the anti-Saddam side, and almost mad not to be on the anti-war side. But it isn't about taking sides. It's a matter of morality and common sense. To invade another country without international backing through the UN, is immoral, short-sighted and sets a dangerous precedent, however cruel the government under attack. The special tragedy over Iraq is that the anarchic outcome was predictable and predicted, and the allies did far too little to anticipate and prevent it. As far as Britain is concerned, the failure to find weapons of mass destruction merely removes the fig leaf from a policy that has had more to do with paying dues to the Americans than with either 'régime change' or securing peace in the region. The problem now is that to stay in Iraq risks hundreds of allied lives, followed by an ignominious retreat, while to leave precipitously will provoke a bloodbath and the installation of another oppressive government. Better not start from here.

26 September 2003

Harold Pinter

1. The invasion of Iraq was simply yet another monstrous assertion of American power and British subservience to that power. Weapons of mass destruction? Rubbish. Liberation of the Iraqi people? Rubbish. The invasion demonstrated utter contempt for the concept of international law and has

brought about the death of thousands, anarchy and chaos. The invasion was a gangster act, a further step towards US domination of the world and control of the world's resources. But in this case it's not working.
2. Quite obviously the opposite – in spades.

19 September 2003

John Press

My dominant, and conflicting, emotions about the American-led invasion of Iraq in March and April 2003 are joy at the fall of Saddam Hussein and sorrow at yet another phase of suffering inflicted on the people of Iraq. The fallibility of Intelligence and its manipulation by the British government serve as a reminder that politics is a dirty game. My tentative verdict is that the invasion was, in the classic phrase, worse than a crime, a blunder.

The Middle East is an abstraction, like the Near East (which has mysteriously disappeared). In 1919 the victorious Allies carved up the old Turkish Empire and fabricated a number of new States in the hope that this would advance their own economic and strategic interests. For more than eighty years most of the region has been ruled by dictators who were corrupt or brutal or both. There seems little hope that things will get better during the next eighty years.

18 September 2003

Kathleen Raine

I believe that war never solves anything; although if ever war was justified it was probably the war against Nazi Germany. But the rise of the Nazis was itself in part the result of the punitive peace terms imposed on Germany by Lloyd George and Clemenceau after the First World War.

I was against the American military action against Saddam Hussein which was illegal and hypocritical. Saddam Hussein was no doubt a tyrant but America's motives were mot the liberation of the Iraqi people but the intention to secure control of Iraqi oil.

Far from bringing about peace or stability in the region, the war, in which cluster-bombs and other weapons of atrocity were used – while the Americans themselves did not mind how many innocent Iraqis were killed but themselves expected their own casualties to number mere hundreds – the war will have de-stabilized the region, made enemies of the Islamic world as a whole for America and also Great Britain who stood 'shoulder to shoulder' with the aggressor, President Bush, acting against the advice of the United Nations, the will of the British people, even the Pope. The devastation in Iraq is nothing to the American aggressors, and they are likely to continue their aggressive policy in order to attain world domination and impose the 'American way of life' – so-called democracy – on the Islamic world. America has not learned the bitter lesson of 11 September. For the British to support the present American regime – illegally elected in the first place – is foolish and incomprehensible and inexcusable. It is not likely that Mr Bush's regime will reward Mr Blair for his support . . .

Now deliberately the Western nations seem to be working towards Armageddon, building up 'weapons of mass destruction' (our most profitable export) on a scale unimaginable by Iraq or any of her neighbouring Arab countries. But we are preparing the downfall of Western supremacy also.

8 May 2003

Frederic Raphael

Any practical action against Saddam would have to be American-led. Hence to be against American leadership is to be in favour of leaving Saddam to enjoy the wealth and power which he had obtained through banditry. To be 'against war' is a worthy sentiment (which I share), but a useless policy. The Sybarites were against war, and were destroyed by the Crotoniotes, who were nastier, but were not. Hedonism is nice, but it is no recipe for survival in a nasty world. Morality does not supply political answers either: morals are static, politics dynamic.

War kills; so can peace: sanctions were supposed to avoid war, but provoked more deaths – as we were often reminded – than military action did. If an action is more virtuous according to the number of lives it saves, then the US action was preferable to UN sanctions, which allowed Saddam to starve his people, and blame the West, while living in gross luxury, funding terrorism and murdering those who murmured against him.

It may be noble to oppose war 'on principle', but making it an absolute evil outlaws any attempt ever to overthrow a murderous regime. If human lives are 'sacred', regimes are not. The moralists' definition of Saddam's Iraq as a sovereign state with implicit rights to run its own affairs (and murder factories) belongs to the realm of politics, not of morals. No absolute right sanctions those who run a state, with no mandate but force, to kill 'their' citizens. Saddam Hussein was a murderer and so were those around him. Their ejection from power, and from access to enormous wealth and from the potency which goes with it, can hardly be objectionable *morally*. Nor does not the moral fallibility of a policeman make the arrest of a killer less justifiable. Even hypocrites can do the right thing.

If it is true that Saddam did not (yet) have WMD on the scale we were promised, it is no great matter: he clearly wanted them, had the means to procure them and would, without much doubt, have accelerated their production if, after being on the start line, the Americans had been impelled, by 'the world community' or anti-capitalist humbug or their own timidity, to withdraw. No great power could have backed down in the circumstances. It was because those who wish Western society no good longed for America's hegemony to be broken that they paraded Saddam as the victim of an injustice. He lived by the sword and, if he is dead, he died by it. Some wring their hands; others applaud. I know which hands I should sooner shake.

Did the no-war faction suppose that Saddam Hussein contributed to the stability and peacefulness of the Middle East? Did such people think the same thing in 1991? Did many, or any, of them ever acknowledge that it was adherence to the strict letter of the UN mandate that halted the US and other forces in the Gulf War and so left Saddam Hussein to enjoy his stolen property for another twelve years?

The notion that the UN was a determining, let alone a wise, force in moral and political matters is an illusion which only those opposed to the United States could press with any sincerity. France, Germany and Russia form a curious oracle to consult about moral propriety. How many people have died in Chechnya and how many German or French diplomats have protested?

As to the second question, who can know what will bring 'lasting peace and stability'? If you pitch the demand for certainty and enduring consequences high enough, no human action can be justified; with regard to the future, all is uncertain except Ben Franklin's famous duo, but some results are likelier than others. Put the issue a different way – 'Is there good reason to think that if we could achieve playback and return affairs to where they stood after 9/11/01, but before March 2003, the Middle East would be (more) likely to be lastingly peaceful and stable?' – and the answer becomes less problematic. I have no wish to return to the *status quo ante*, with Saddam vindicated in his insolence, secure in his tyranny and available to fund terror, and with his weapons programme, with the almost boundless oil revenues which French and German and Russian connivance would almost certainly allow him to enjoy. Who does favour this?

The overthrow of Saddam will probably do some good; it may not. His resurrection or restoration would not, on any account, be a huge help in the pious search for justice, peace and all the other things which men sometimes agree to settle for when they can't get their way by force, bluff or money.

30 May 2003

Piers Paul Read

As a Roman Catholic I believe that a war is only just if it is undertaken in self-defence. I did not believe for a moment, despite the government's propaganda about weapons of mass destruction, that the Iraqi armed forces posed a threat to the United Kingdom or its vital interests: therefore the invasion of Iraq by US and British forces was unjust. It is an irony that Bush and Blair, who profess to be Christians, ignored the advice of almost all the Christian leaders, among them Pope John Paul II, that it would be wrong to invade Iraq.

Will the occupation of Iraq bring stability to the Middle East? Only if a *pax Americana* leads to the establishment of a viable Palestinian state.

13 June 2003

William Rees-Mogg

[In response to our questionnaire, Lord Rees-Mogg invited us to quote from one of his columns in *The Times*. The following piece is taken from his article in that newspaper dated 3 March 2003.]

In Iraq, genocide has continued, particularly against two ethnic groups, the Kurds and the Marsh Arabs, for more than 20 years. It is still continuing. If Saddam Hussein survives, he can be expected to redouble the killing, as happened aftr 1991. The anti-war activists need to reflect on the murderous consequences of their policies.

Three speeches in last Wednesday's fascinating parliamentary debates need to be studied. One was Lord Goodhart's, which discussed the issue in respect of international law. The other two were Ann Clwyd's in the House of Commons [*Hansard*, 26 February] and Baroness Nicholson's in the House of Lords [ibid.].

Ann Clwyd spoke from her experience of the genocide against the Kurds, Lady Nicholson from her similar experience of the genocide against the Marsh Arabs. Anyone who wants to have a serious understanding of the issues has a duty to read these speeches. Ann Clwyd's speech had a great impact on the House of Commons and on the press; House of Lords speeches attract less attention, but Lady Nicholson's was no less important. Their case was unanswerable and unanswered.

First of all one needs to consider what international law says about intervention to stop genocide. Lady Nicholson asserted that 'the duty on state parties to the genocide convention is to stop the genocide and to punish those engaged in this ethnic mass murder. If the Security Council cannot be persuaded to act, an operation should be mounted by any signatory to the convention to secure the perpetrators and bring them to trial . . . Has genocide been committed against the Marsh Arabs? Yes; then action is imperative.'

Lady Nicholson sits as a Liberal Democrat and she was therefore speaking against the pacifist line of her party. Lord Goodhart, who is a highly respected international lawyer, stayed with his party's anti-war line. That adds weight to his legal opinion in support of the right to intervene. He summed up the state of the law in this way: 'Let us look first at humanitarian intervention. This is a new principle which has risen outside the charter. It was most clearly recognized in Kosovo. It is widely, but not universally, accepted by international lawyers. In cases such as genocide by rulers against their own people, as in Rwanda and Cambodia, it is hard to deny that such a principle exists.'

This does represent a change. The traditional post-1945 view was that sovereign governments were free to abuse their own people, to torture or kill them, and that no other country could intervene. Kosovo, the trial of Milosevic, the conventions on torture and on genocide, and the House of Lords judgement on General Pinochet, have created a much wider right in international law to intervene for humanitarian reasons.

Lord Goodhart went on to argue that Saddam Hussein, though 'a murderous tyrant' who has killed 'thousands of his opponents', has not gone quite far enough to qualify under this doctrine. 'The closest Saddam Hussein has come to this is in his treatment of the Marsh Arabs, whose culture he had destroyed and many of whose people he has killed. But it would be unrealistic to treat even that as a justification for war.' Lord Goodhart spoke before Lady Nicholson; had he been speaking after her, he could hardly have made the case that Saddam Hussein's genocide was only a little one.

The important point is that, as a lawyer, Lord Goodhart confirms that a right to intervene on humanitarian grounds is now internationally recognized.

It would be hard to argue that Saddam Hussein is a less serious case than Milosevic.

Ann Clwyd's speech destroyed the argument that Saddam Hussein belongs only to the junior league of genocidal tyrants. She pointed out that, before 1991, the victims already included 'Arabs as well as Kurds. They include Assyrians, Turkomans and the Shias in the south'. She referred to the evidence of Human Rights Watch and Amnesty International, as well as the 'documents from the torture centre' captured by the Kurds. On her latest visit she had opened, on Kurdish territory, the first genocide museum in Iraq.

She gave the evidence of a young Iraqi who had spoken to her within the past few days. He had been held in the Abu Ghraib prison in Baghdad. 'He said that almost every day people were executed at that prison – not one person, but hundreds. When there was an attack on Uday Hussein's life some time ago, 2,000 prisoners were executed on the same day.'

Ann Clwyd also recently visited a UN camp in the Kurdish area where there were hundreds of current victims of ethnic cleansing, which 'goes on all the time'. Even so, Lord Goodhart may be right in thinking that the Marsh Arabs have been massacred on an even greater scale. Lady Nicholson observed that: 'The massacre of the North Kurds is well known in the West and internationally accepted as genocide. But I claim that in contrast the Iraq regime's long planned and near finalized extinction of the indigenous inhabitants of the Lower Mesopotamian marshlands of Iraq has gone virtually unnoticed.'

She asserts that: 'Four million people have fled Iraq.' Surely, four million is a large enough number to qualify for humanitarian intervention?

Brian Sewell

1. Against.
2. No, neither.

15 June 2003

Alan Sillitoe

I was in favour of the war in Iraq. Let me quote a poem by the great John Milton, called 'The End of Violent Men':

> Oh, how comely it is and how reviving
> To the Spirits of just men long opprest!
> When God into the hands of their deliverer
> Puts invincible might
> To quell the might of the Earth, th' oppressour,
> The brute and boist'rous force of violent men . . .
> He all their Ammunition
> And feats of War defeats
> With plain Heroic magnitude of mind . . .
> Their Armories and Magazins contemns,
> Renders them useless, while
> With winged expedition
> Swift as the lightning glance he executes
> His errand on the wicked, who surpris'd
> Lose their defence distracted and amaz'd.

Who could put it better than that? One can only congratulate the United States forces, and the soldiers of Great Britain.

And, as for settling things in the Middle East, if this won't help the process nothing will. Israel and the West must stick together.

8 May 2003

Robert Skidelsky

I opposed the war against Iraq, because I took the view that Saddam Hussein was no threat to his neighbours. I argued in the magazine *Prospect* (February 2003) that most of his weapons of mass destruction had been eliminated during and after the Gulf War and that a combination of sanctions and UN inspectors could prevent him from rebuilding his supply. He could thus be kept 'bottled up' in Baghdad till he died or was overthrown internally. It would be costly to maintain external pressure on him, but less costly than war which, in addition, would have unpredictable consequences for the Middle East as a whole.

Since then we have had the war, Saddam is gone, and American and British armies occupy Iraq. Hardly any international lawyer believes the war was legal; no one has found any weapons of mass destruction. The serious question is whether the British Prime Minister lied or was simply deceived in asserting that Iraq had a large stock of these weapons.

We would at least be making progress if we recognized that the avowed reasons for the war were fraudulent. This would clear the ground for an urgent debate about the future of international relations. The post-war system was based on the doctrine of national sovereignty. We now need to ask: is this doctrine now obsolete? If so, can we define the scope of justifiable military intervention in the internal affairs of states? If so, how can we amend the UN Charter in such a way as to make such interventions legal in international law?

If we can get agreements on these matters, the Iraqi war will have done some good. This does not mean we should have started it, since the end never justifies the means.

1 June 2003

D.J. Taylor

I believe that Saddam Hussein was (or is) an evil man – evil in the ancient, Biblical sense – who deserved to be deposed. Whether George Bush, who has some claims to be regarded as the shiftiest political operator on the planet, was entitled to effect his overthrow is another question.

I also believe that my opinion on this subject is of no interest to anyone, and that the days when writers could be expected usefully to contribute to political debates beyond the immediate sphere of their writing are altogether gone.

5 November 2003

Emma Tennant

I was opposed to the American-led intervention against Saddam Hussein's regime, because it had more 'for' than 'against' in it: for oil, for domination; and by insisting (illegally) on this path it came to resemble the regime it had declared itself against.

As Robin Cook said on 10 July 2003, 'This was a war made in Washington, pushed by a handful of neo-Conservatives and pursued for reasons of US foreign strategy and domestic politics. What made this war inevitable was not an increased threat from Iraq, but a regime change in the US.'

The intervention has proved a disaster already, with killing and political instability the order of the day.

11 July 2003

Studs Terkel

The pre-emptive strike against Iraq was really an assault upon our native intelligence and whatever sense of decency we still possess. It now turns out – as though we didn't know it beforehand – based on an outrageous lie – and will, if anything, encourage 'terrorism' and imperil what chances we may have for world peace.

There is only one course for us Americans to take – an old-fashioned one: Turn the scoundrels out. This applies to your chieftain, Tony Blair, who has played Jeeves to a doltish Bertie W.— our (God help us) appointed chieftain, George W.

16 July 2003

Paul Theroux

1, Utterly against military action.
2. Peace and stability in the Middle East might be possible when Israel withdraws from the land it has illegally occupied and tried to colonize since 1967; when a political (not military) solution is found to resolve the conflict; and a viable Palestinian state is established.

7 October 2003

D.M. Thomas

I would much rather trust the views of taxi-drivers on any matter of great political importance than those of writers and intellectuals. History shows that the latter almost always get it wrong. The Falklands War is a good recent example. I was one of a mere handful of writers contributing to *Authors Take Sides on the Falklands* who supported the action. In the event, that war freed the islanders from a tyrannous occupation; delivered a lesson to aggressors; and destroyed the wicked Argentinian *junta* in favour of democracy. The people of Britain, who supported the war by a large majority, were right; the authors, wrong.

I have felt no such certainty about the war in Iraq. Both for and against there were strong arguments. It always seemed unlikely that Saddam Hussein could be a threat to us; and so how could we justify an invasion of a sovereign country? I believe that the sovereignty of individual nations is a guarantee of liberty for all, against the very real threat of liberal fascism. I was opposed to NATO's interference over Kosovo, for that reason.

Nonetheless, in the case of Iraq, this was an evil regime, responsible for millions of deaths. I was impressed by Ann Clwyd's quiet but passionate witnessing to Saddam's horrors. A war would, in the end, save lives, and give freedom from fear to millions who had never known it, and who had otherwise no prospect of it. One had to trust one's leaders – now, it seems, mistakenly – that Iraq had weapons of mass destruction; but for me this carried much less weight than the monstrousness of the regime. I felt too that Blair's conviction was – for once – convincing; that a man of sincere Christian faith would not make himself responsible for death and destruction without good reason. There are times when one simply has to trust one's country's leaders, who know more of the facts than we do.

So I supported the war, and still do; firmly, though never without self-doubt. When France and Germany came out against it, I became a stronger supporter of war. An alliance of Britain and the USA has always been for the world's good; whereas Germany and France standing together reminded me too much of Vichy.

I certainly don't believe that intervention will bring lasting peace and stability in the region. Only justice for the Palestinians can bring any hope of that.

24 May 2003

William Trevor

1. Against.
2. No. It will make peace and stability infinitely more difficult to establish.

28 June 2003

Terry Waite

In my heart of hearts I would like to be a pacifist but I am not. There are times when I believe that the use of force may be justified but only after every alternative has been explored to the limit. Even then I have strong reservations as in modern warfare the main victims are so often women and children. It is all very well military experts attempting to soothe us by speaking about 'targeted' bombing. Physical injury may be avoided but the trauma suffered by innocent victims is dreadful and all too often remains a burden for life.

'It is comparatively easy, given sufficient resources, to rebuild roads and bridges,' said a UN representative to me in Kosovo. 'It is much more difficult to rebuild traumatized young lives. There are just not the skilled people around to do that job.' Warfare must be the absolute last resort.

Although at the time of writing the war has been over for some weeks I have not changed my tune. I hold no brief whatsoever for the evil regime formerly dominating Iraq. However, in March I said publicly that I did not believe every option had been explored and that the Americans, with the British and a few other stragglers in tow, were intent on going to war before the weather became unbearably hot. Although I could not prove it, I felt reasonably sure in my own mind that the reasons put forward for engaging were not the main reasons. I continue to suspect that the principal reasons were economic as they so often are in most international conflicts. A powerful military power such as America does not choose to invade Iraq out of altruistic motive alone. As for the argument that Britain and possibly the USA were in grave danger of imminent attack, this was almost certainly a fiction. Where are the weapons – biological or otherwise? Even if these are found eventually, where are the means of delivery?

Military might will not resolve the problems that face the Middle East and indeed face the whole world. Lasting peace and stability is a goal that we should continue to strive for even though it may never be fully achieved. This latest excursion into warfare has confirmed the view held by many throughout the world that America is set on securing her own economic empire regardless of the cost to the poor of this world. Sadly, I suspect that Britain has danced along to the tune of death largely for her own economic reasons.

The world is changing before our eyes. We are witnessing the demise of the Nation State and the emergence of States where the market rules. Competitiveness and occasionally brutality are consequential to such a development. It is distasteful to me for these realities to be larded over with a profession of high moral intent.

If the great market states of this world were truly intent on building a just moral order for all nations, then greater effort would be put into reforming the United Nations and creating an international structure that would move us towards justice for all. It is not beyond the wit of men and women to build mechanisms that would enable a reformed United Nations to find new ways of dealing with rogue states. Such a body probably demands that which is seen by some to be politically impossible – the sacrificing of a certain amount of National self interest. It is alarming, to say the least, that the United States appears to have turned away from such an ideal by rejecting the International Court of Justice: by refusing to sign the Kyoto agreement and by holding prisoners in a manner that many deem to be illegal. Such behaviour fuels the fire of hatred that motivates some who would engage in acts of terrorism.

Iraq and the surrounding region remain in deep trouble which will not be resolved by military force or foreign domination. The situation is utterly complex and cannot be summarized in a few words. Perhaps I yearn for the impossible when I ask for political leaders from all nations to have the courage to be truthful: the wisdom to make a deeper analysis together and the compassion to remember that the grief of a poor mother in the Middle East is just the same as the grief of her more affluent sister elsewhere.

12 June 2003

Arnold Wesker

Eleven years ago, distressed by the Serb attacks on the Bosnians, I wrote an article printed in *The Guardian* (6 August 11992) as 'The remedy that humanity deserves' ('International Benign Force' was my title) in which I promulgated two arguments.

First: the need to re-definition the concept of 'sovereignty'. No state, I argued, may be deemed a sovereign state unless its leaders have been democratically elected. If the notion of sovereignty involves the notion of respect for a people's way of life within its territory, then that people must have been free to decide upon that way of life, and not be living a life imposed upon them. A nation's 'sovereignty' can be deemed infringed even if that infringement has been enacted by a handful of its own tyrannical citizens.

The second argument argued for the creation of an international benign force to help free those people from their tyranny.
The United Nations Charter says that military action can be taken if there is a humanitarian crisis. Robin Cook confirmed this in his House of Commons resignation speech when he pointed out that the UK intervened militarily in Kosovo because 'there was a humanitarian crisis'.

I submit that when a tyrant emerges who usurps the sovereignty of his own people then the ensuing corruption and brutality and denial of human rights constitutes a humanitarian crisis.

This is what I understood to be the Iraqi situation, and for that reason I supported military intervention by the coalition to which end, before the war began, I wrote the following ironically scathing letter to *The Guardian*, 4 February 2003:

'If I were Saddam Hussein I'd be glowing with pride and pleasure, to say nothing of relief.

"Here I am, a tyrant who has usurped the sovereignty of his own people; who has murdered many of them; who has invaded two of his neighbours, and look! I've turned the world upside down: I've divided Europe, I've put Nato in disarray, I've got American and British forces on my doorstep wasting billions of dollars to do nothing, the stock market has fallen to its lowest in ages, the American economy is faltering and the UK is not doing too well, either. I've got the leading artists and intellectuals of Europe and America to march and sign petitions helping me to perpetuate the tyrannical oppression of my people, I've got lovely people from all over coming to Baghdad to act as human shields against military attack so I don't need to waste Iraqi lives doing it, and best of all I've got both Osama bin Laden calling for suicide attacks against my enemies, and Harold Pinter writing verses against my enemies."

'Oppressors could never have had it so good!'

The only development that would make me think the military intervention had been a mistake is if Iraq became an Islamic theocracy. One tyranny would then have been exchanged for another.

15 May 2003

A.N. Wilson

Before the war, both sides exaggerated. Advocates of unilateral Anglo-American action said the threat of nuclear or chemical attack by Saddam was imminent. We now know it wasn't. Anti-war demonstrators, including myself, thought there might be huge battles, vast civilian casualties. In fact, although casualties (figures as yet undisclosed on 15 September) are considerable, the Americans did achieve a victory with remarkably small loss of life, and rid Iraq, and the Middle East of a criminal, murderous thug.

It is too soon to say, whether the unstable situation in Iraq, and in the entire region, has been made worse by the removal of a terrible dictator. Mr Blair promised the Iraqis that the West would give aid to rebuild the nation's infrastructure, and help schools, hospitals, etc. So far this hasn't happened. I do not feel it is fitting for Western writers to answer this question – ask the Iraqis. As an Englishman I did not feel it was my war, and I did not believe bilateral without UN support was justified. If I were an Iraqi, I might be feeling glad that Saddam Hussein had been overthrown, but I might also wish the Western troops would leave me to run my own country, or conduct my own quarrels. I'd know that all the powers – Russia, France, Britain, America, who dispute my country were really wanting to make money out of the Iraqi oil wells.

15 September 2003

Authors Take Sides on the Gulf War

Preface

to *Authors Take Sides on the Gulf War*

The Iraqi invasion of Kuwait, which precipitated the Gulf War, took place on 2 August 1990. Less than a week later 'Operation Desert Shield' began, with two US aircraft carriers, a battleship, a troopship and a battalion of marines sailing for the Persian Gulf. The multinational Coalition's military build-up in the region continued. On America's Thanksgiving Day, 20 November, President George Bush Snr visited the troops in Saudi Arabia and the same day the UN approved military action if an ultimatum calling on Iraq to withdraw from Kuwait was ignored.

That ultimatum expired on 15 January 1991. The allied offensive, 'Desert Storm', began the following day with the dropping of thousands of tons of explosives on Iraq and the aerial bombardment continued until 24 February when land operations began before dawn: US, British and French troops, under the UN flag, entered Kuwait and Iraq.

The questionnaire, on which the pages that follow are based, was posted to authors over a period of a fortnight from 25 February to 7 March 1991. When we started to send it out, politicians and the media were predicting a long struggle. In the event, however, the land offensive in the Gulf lasted less than 100 hours and our circular reached most authors at about the time Bush Snr announced that hostilities would cease as from 6 a.m. on 28 February. Some of those authors we approached who failed to respond may well have thought that, with the end of the war, the book would be cancelled.

As it happened, the book *was* cancelled, but not due to the cessation of hostilities: a major house-fire delayed publication to the point where its relevance was put in doubt. With the advent of a second war against Iraq, the opportunity has presented itself to publish the results of the earlier survey. It will, we believe, enable illuminating comparisons to be made.

In re-reading the responses to the Gulf War, it seems to us important to stress that they were written either immediately, or shortly after the event. All the authors were able to do was to express their views in the light of the knowledge available, by comparison with replies to the Iraq war questionnaire which cover a much longer period, in many cases giving the authors the benefit of hindsight.

As with Vietnam, the Falklands, and the Iraq conflicts, the Gulf War was a difficult issue and one which divided friends, families, political parties and the countries involved in the Coalition. Before the fighting began Britain itself was very deeply divided on the use of force. On 11 December 1990, when the House of Commons voted on the issue, MPs were 10 to 1 in favour of the Government, for a UN resolution bringing it to the point where force would be used. Yet on the same day, Gallup conducted a poll which showed that only 31% of the nation believed that force should be used. Shortly before the UN deadline expired, in January 1991, *The Daily Telegraph* suggested that less than half the country favoured the use of force. The replies received to our questionnaire on the subject indicated that slightly less than half the authors approached supported the Gulf War.

The two questions we asked were:

Are you for, or against, the use of armed force in liberating Kuwait?
How, in your opinion, can lasting peace and stability be restored to the Middle East?

The Answers

The Questions

Are you for, or against, the use of armed force in liberating Kuwait?

How, in your opinion, can lasting peace and stability be restored to the Middle East?

The Answers

Paul Ableman

Many authors, and indeed reflective people of all kinds, are emotional pacifists. They believe that, in Shelley's magnificent formulation: 'Those who kill in uniform merely add the ignominy of servitude to the crime of murder'. They hope that if it ever came to a choice between killing or dying for a belief they would have the courage to choose the latter. I adhere to these values.

Moreover, many of us would maintain that so far from being a whimsical affectation such an attitude can be an effective way of bringing about major political change. The advance and final triumph of Christianity and the liberation of India from British rule are two important demonstrations of its power. It is, however, doubtful if non-violence can be considered an absolute imperative in the unique situation of our age. The essence of this is that our science and technology has outstripped our social and political organization. We still administer the planet in terms of the obsolete premise that 'sovereign' states have little or no organic connection with the greater planetary environment. In reality, of course, our technology, in peace as in war, knows no frontiers. Not only the threat posed by nuclear weapons but the hope offered by global administration of things like energy provision, distribution of raw materials, protection of threatened resources like water, forests and the atmosphere underline the desirability of a world administration. A non-violent movement aimed at this might ultimately prove successful. But the grim fact is that we cannot afford the decades, or probably more, that such a campaign would require since a nuclear conflict could break out at any time and terminate not only human, but, in certain scenarios, biological history.

It was in the light of such considerations that I applauded the use of armed force for liberating Kuwait. It seemed to me that military intervention by America would be the best way of eliminating the nuclear threat posed by an Iraq having an advanced nuclear weapons programme and led by an utterly unscrupulous military dictator. I was both appalled and bewildered when President Bush stopped short of ensuring this goal and indeed of achieving any very useful result beyond the – admittedly desirable – removal of Iraqi forces from Kuwait soil. It is questionable, according to international lawyers, if his restraint was strictly in agreement with the UN resolution. It is beyond doubt that it precipitated vastly more suffering – the martyrdom of a substantial part of the Kurdish nation – than it alleviated. Common sense, compassion, vision, military logic all conspire to insist that General Schwarzkopf should have been allowed to continue his campaign for the few extra days needed to take him into Baghdad and put Saddam Hussein in the dock for a Nuremberg-type trial in which the charge sheet should have contained the additional indictment of 'crimes against the planet'. The bizarre and loathsome spectacle of a tyrant waging war, and presiding over attempted genocide, *after* his defeat by the supposed forces of decency and humanity offers little encouragement to the view that a new maturity can be perceived in international relations. It also makes the relevant Western leaders, who contracted in the space of days from valiant crusaders to quaking isolationists, seem not only contemptible but surreal. But the tragic farce has at least had the virtue of demonstrating once again the inexaggerably important truth that the most desirable characteristic of any politician is his or her susceptibility to being chucked out.

The Middle East, which is the turbulent confluence of three of the world's major religions, Christianity, Judaism and Islam, and a much greater number of racial groups varying from Mongolian to Caucasian and Negroid to Semitic, is clearly a global hot spot. The truth is, of course, that there is unlikely to be 'lasting peace and stability' anywhere in the world until a world government is instituted. But even by normative standards the Middle East, inflamed by its vast oil treasure, is bound to remain disorderly. I personally accept the view that the chief hope for restraining the region's potential for violent eruption is the provision of an acceptable modus vivendi between Israel and its neighbours. What commends itself to me, however, as the best way of achieving this would stand little chance of adoption. This would call for mankind in general to accept that religious systems are poetic metaphors and not records of historical events. With this established, the Jews, in exchange for no longer being stigmatized 'God-killers', could formally renounce the claim to being 'God's chosen people'. It is little recognized, even by Jews themselves, how much of the animosity directed towards them is based on this preposterous and obsolete claim. If it were, like the 'God-killer' absurdity, consigned to the realm of myth where both belong then the way would be opened for co-operation and an ultimate Middle Eastern commonwealth.

Failing any such solution, which must, alas, be considered Utopian as yet, the best hope for reasonable stability in the region is doubtless an augmented United Nations supervision, probably chiefly implemented by American economic and armed power, in an attempt to keep the peace and prevent both proliferation of nuclear weapons in the area and the use of those which already exist.

The 'pax Americana' has made a shaky start, which the Kurds will justifiably anathematize to the end of their history, but it still probably offers the most realistic hope of moving towards, and ultimately achieving, a world administration. On a planet menaced by a global technology this is probably the *sine qua non* of long-term survival.

25 April 1991

Dannie Abse

With changing circumstances my views have changed. I don't think I have anything original to say. Like so many others I'm sickened by the whole thing.

Bertrand Russell wrote 'The reason that Hobbes gives for supporting the State, namely that it is the only alternative to anarchy, is in the main a valid one.' He went on to say though, 'A State may, however, be so bad that temporary anarchy seems preferable to its continuance, as in France in 1789 and in Russia in 1917'.

Bush and his advisers evidently believe Saddam Hussein is better than anarchy and what would come out of it. Most of us simply don't know and despair.

22 May 1991

Richard Adams

You ask me two questions. The answer to the first is that I am unequivocally and totally in favour of the use of armed force in liberating Kuwait. You will probably have seen General Sir John Hackett's letter in *The Times* of today's date. My views agree entirely with his, and I would only add that, having myself lived as an adolescent through the 1930s and experienced the weak-kneed reaction of 'the men of Munich' to Hitler and the ineffectiveness of the League of Nations, I can only rejoice that the United Nations should have taken so firm, unanimous and effective a stand against the brutal tyrant Saddam Hussein.

Secondly, you ask me how, in my opinion, lasting peace and stability can be restored in the middle east. This is, of course, an enormous question and I cannot possibly deal with it at length. However, I will say this. The core of the trouble in the middle east is Israel. All the Arab countries are at one in their bitter enmity towards Israel. Israel is, in effect, an American colony. It is not, in itself, a going economic concern. It has no minerals, no river power and no deep-sea ports. I strongly suspect that it exists to a very large extent upon American subsidies. When one goes to America, one is struck by the virtual totality of the support for Israel and the general hostility to Islam. What has got to happen is that America and the Americans must learn to recognize, to respect and, in plain terms, to understand and like Islam. We have a point of hope here in Russia. The west is very anxious to further good relations with Russia and everyone rejoices at the end of the Cold War. Russia has a number of Islamic constituent states in the south. One does not know, of course, what is the future of the Soviet Union and whether these states will remain within it, but nevertheless there is a degree of respect in Russia for Islam which the USA would do well to explore more fully. At the moment, Islam's hatred of Israel seems an almost insoluble problem, but nevertheless, if trouble in the middle east is to be resolved and averted for the future, this is the problem which must be solved. It cannot and should not be resolved by force of arms, and therefore it must be resolved by understanding and friendship.

The other feature in the middle east causing trouble to the west is Colonel Gaddafi's Libya. However, I see this as less troublesome. Gaddafi has not got the active support of other Arab states and the threat that he represents can be controlled by the threat of force. He is obviously afraid of the western powers and only goes as far as he dares. It is to be hoped that his regime will in due course be superseded. A conference between the western and eastern powers might well have on its agenda something about limiting the activities of Libya.

27 February 1991

Fleur Adcock

It was this disgusting and, in the end, useless war which finally destroyed any lingering hopes I might have had for the future of humanity.

I see not the slightest chance that lasting peace and stability can ever be restored to the Middle East – or, indeed, to the world in general.

6 May 1991

John Adlard

The expedition to the Gulf was an act of folly. Whatever military victories we achieve, it will remain an act of folly. In London during the past few years I have been meeting Muslim students from nations covering the whole distance between the Atlantic and the Indian Ocean, and among them Islam is an unfailing bond. Our religion seems in decay, theirs is full of life; our imperial past and oil-obsessed present make us deeply suspect. We need to earn the friendship and respect of those nations. This will not be done by restoring to the Sabah family a state that is practically their private property. We have already made the undesirable Saddam Hussein into a hero for many Muslims, and Edward Said is not alone in his 'outraged grief' at the destruction of Baghdad.

How, in our squalid island, can we spare the money for such an adventure? Our citizens are too poor to keep open the public libraries, or even the public lavatories. But it will be money well spent for a generation who, having sloughed off socialism, are thrilled by markets and wars.

We would best promote peace and stability in the Middle East if we were to forego our profits from a cynical arms trade and keep our forces well away from the area. What would the readers of our tabloids think if vast Arab armies, bristling with sophisticated weaponry, surged up the Volga, to come to the aid of Lithuania?

28 February 1991

Joan Aiken

The Gulf War should never have happened. So long as rich Western nations such as the USA and Germany continue to make and export arms, regardless of whose hands they fall into, wars like this one will continue to erupt, because the makers and purchasers have to find a use for their products. Wars will not stop until there is a total ban on armaments manufacture . . . what a hopeless ideal. The Gulf War was inevitable; and the fact that the arms used in it were so horribly successful will only give the proponents an excuse to start preparing for another.

27 February 1991

Shabbir Akhtar

I am against the use of armed force to liberate Kuwait only because Western outrage at illegal and immoral occupation in that district is selective. Saddam Hussein did not invent the idea of annexation. The Gulf War was a conflict over vested western interests. For Britain, it was also a psychologically necessary war: How dare an Arab chap alter boundaries erected, admittedly arbitrarily, by an Englishman? (For British people, the discovery of North Sea oil was a religious event: it showed that God was not an Arab and might be English after all, notwithstanding His rough justice and even rougher sense of humour.)

The Church of England behaved immorally in supporting the war. But it is, after all, the most profitable of our nationalized industries! So, let's not be too harsh. In any case, it is a fortunate feature of divine grace that it allows faith to be total even where truth is partial.

Islam and the West can co-exist once Westerners recognize that Muslims want to live with the West, not under it. That is the first lesson in the first year of the Hot War.

14 March 1991

Walter Allen

I was for the use of armed force in liberating Kuwait and am still amazed at the skill and apparent ease with which the war was executed by the allies.

Whether a lasting peace can be established in the Middle East seems to me anyone's guess. Certainly it cannot be unless Saddam topples.

7 March 1991

A. Alvarez

From the beginning, the war in the Gulf seemed to me to be just and justifiable, as well as necessary. Of course it was about oil, but the left was, as usual, both childish and dishonest to pretend that only the interests of the profligate, gas-guzzling nations were being protected. Everyone's economic survival was at stake – that of the second and third world nations, as well as the first. Had Saddam Hussein not been stopped when he took over Kuwait, he would have moved on into Saudi Arabia. At that point, the control of about half of the world's oil supplies would have been in the hands of a genocidal dictator with biological weapons, a nuclear potential and vast territorial ambitions – a thug whose domestic rule, by terror and omnipresent secret police, was modelled, like his paranoid behaviour, on that of his hero, Stalin. I can think of no sane argument for sitting still and allowing that to happen.

I am glad the coalition held together and turned the Gulf War into precisely the kind of operation the United Nations was originally set up for: that is, an international police action in which the USA was a major player not because of any imperialist ambitions but because it is the UN's most powerful military force. This style of concerted operation would not have been possible before perestroika because the USSR would automatically have taken the opposite side and turned the occasion into a confrontation between the superpowers. The fact that this did not happen gives me hope for the future. Also, the effectiveness of the action – the speed, skill, efficiency and strategic brilliance of the allied forces, as well as their extraordinarily low casualty-rate – may perhaps discourage the next bully with territorial ambitions.

I am far less hopeful about the prospects for stability in the Middle East. It has never happened before and I can see no good reason for it to happen now. What does seem important is not to inflame Arab sensibilities any further, which means we should be seen to get out. If there has to be a western military presence it should be naval, not land-based. Since the Arab states have played a significant role in the war, we should encourage them to make their own arrangements for peace and to police the area themselves, while we confine ourselves to the traditional non-violent means of persuasion we are so good at: diplomacy, bribery and economic blackmail. In the meantime, the best strategy is to keep a low profile and resign ourselves to the fact that they are going to hate us whatever we do.

12 March 1991

Mulk Raj Anand

Greetings! from the midst of a despair in which I have been repeating the words of the poet Lorca, 'Agony, agony dream and ferment!'

I think I wrote intensely before the Second World War after I had been to Spain in 1937, and knew that Franco's victory there, with the French and the British imperialists conniving at Hitler and Mussolini, helping Franco. Hitler would soon be on the up and up; and that is what happened after Munich, with Chamberlain coming back saying 'Peace in our time', when everyone knew that appeasement would soon let Hitler take whatever he wanted by force.

I was a conscientious objector, as a pseudo-Gandhian for the first three years of the war, but joined George Orwell as a freelance broadcaster in the Indian section of the BBC after 1942, when Russia was attacked by the Germans. I helped the *Voice* magazine, in which E.M. Forster, Herbert Read, and even T.S. Eliot, came to say, in their own way, what Richard Hillary had said in his book, that we were 'fighting for a half lie against the big lie'. To me, as an Indian victim of Imperialism, it seemed appalling that Churchill should promise freedom in the Atlantic Charter, but not to India. After the war, India did achieve, under the Labour government, transfer of power, though at the cost of partition of the country between a theocratic Pakistan and the secular democracy of India. India decided from then on to remain non-aligned. And promoted the Five Principles of Peace and Co-existence, International Understanding, and Non-participation in any war.

Unfortunately, the greed of the Imperialists, who gave up their colonies, infected the formerly isolationist Americans, coming relatively unscathed through the Second World War, so that many of their industrialists became arms manufacturers. The American democratic state has sought to create tensions all the year round, starting or helping to start a war every now and then, threatening the other super-power, Russia, with a cold war and then the threat of nuclear and atomic weapons and also a star-war . By a strange miracle, Gorbachev forced disarmament, gradual as it was, on the reluctant Americans and thus the enemy Number 1 of the United States disappeared. The problem then was where to sell their armaments.

There are plenty of areas of the world where the Americans could find stooges whose territories, bases and 'spheres of influence' they could use. The Sheikhdoms of the Middle East was one such area, because they are rich in oil. The American century has included them as allies, when they lost their base in Iran following the take-over by fundamentalists. They helped the Sunni, Saddam Hussein, to fight his Muslim Shia neighbour, Iran. Later, when Saddam put on jack-boots, beret and khaki uniform and threw his weight about with a highly trained army and kicked out the Sheikh of Kuwait, the American democrats hustled the UN into challenging his take-over in a short, bloody and highly mechanized war. With a hundred thousand air-raids the Americans levelled large areas of Iraq killing large numbers of the civilian population without any sense of humanity or discrimination.

I can't take sides with either Saddam or the Americans. They are both fighting to control oil prices. I am against all war, being non-violent, or trying to be. I am against India making a nuclear bomb. I feel we should be one country, which will never make a bomb, start a war or commit aggression. Even though America has been giving arms to Pakistan free and conniving at their nefarious designs to make a bomb to attack India, in the interest of the theocratic state they want – Pakistan ('Pak' means Punjab, Afghanistan and Kashmir).

I believe that we should revive the pacifism of Bertrand Russell before the First World War: listen to the still, small voice of Gandhi; see in Gorbachev's iniative, at the cost of the surrender of Socialism, the hope that the bulk of mankind will refuse to be used for the promotion of the American century.

10 March 1991

John Arden

(I wrote for your last publication of this sort – *Authors Take Sides on the Falklands* – I am appalled I have to repeat the process so soon.)

1st March '91: a ceasefire at last; but I have been Against and still *am*. To defeat Saddam Hussein's government by overwhelming force, after enthusiastically supplying him with the means to defeat Kuwait by overwhelming force, brings the circle round to its commencement and promises the same again, somewhere else, the very next time the arms industry sniffs a slack market.

I have no hope that the present coalition of victors (masquerading as the United Nations) can bring peace and stability to the Middle East, I have no hope that they even *wish* to (spoils-grabbing divide-and-rule being far more likely as a future policy). And in any case, what possible answer to your second question should arise from the disgusting ooze of censorship and degraded self-censorship that has seeped all over us throughout the last six months? Whatever is to be done in (and to) the Middle East will be misrepresented to us and we shall not be allowed to learn its full intention until the deception may be seen to have taken a general hold. War levied in defence of UN Resolutions has strangled a crucial section of the UN's own Charter of Human Rights – Article 19, Freedom of Information, Speech, Expression. Our Psy-ops have won a most notable victory, not so much upon Saddam Hussein as over ourselves – 'casualties at a minimum', if you only count Anglo-American soldiers; 'Kuwait liberated', if you don't notice there's hardly any of it left and our speculators are already casting dice for the profits of its reconstruction; 'the hostage-taker and oppressor-of-his-own-people humiliated', after having his own people wantonly held hostage against him by relentless air-bombardment; and 'the *courage* of the allied fliers' magnificently manifest, in contrast to the *cowardice* of (say) the IRA, whose rockets in Whitehall were so heinously fired from no speeding planes but actually in the very next strictly-policed street to their target?

LONG LIVE THE SMOOTHSPEAK OF HALFTRUTH.

LONG LIVE THE GREATBIG LIE.

1 March 1991

Lynne Reid Banks

Before, during and after a war, individuals' attitudes may alter. Mine did—from 55% *for* pre-January 15th, through 51% when the oil slick was released and I lost my nerve about the environmental threat, up to 70% sitting gas-masked in a sealed room in Haifa during an alert, down almost to zero after the retreating Iraqis were subjected to needless overkill on the Basra Road. Now it's 'over', I'm back to 55%.

55% means I was, and am, for it, though not wholeheartedly or with any great gusto. I was for it because I foresaw far worse up the road if Saddam was not stopped. For it because I don't see why *not* having stepped in to reverse or prevent earlier international outrages – Tibet, Afghanistan, the Kurds, etc. ad infinitum – due largely to the constraints of the Cold War, the UN, with an unprecedented degree of unanimity and muscle for once, shouldn't do something firm about this one.

For it because I don't see anything necessarily squalid and unworthy about fighting for essential supplies of something we all depend on, like oil. People always have and they probably always will, until our flawed species finds a better ultimate weapon than force to use against force. What is much more squalid is refusing to fight *unless* you have some vital material interest at stake.

I think one has to be a bit tough-minded in the face of tyranny, instead of whimpering that wars never settle anything. History teaches that some do and some don't. I think this one did, though the cost, as nearly always, was daunting.

As to the future: I was very disturbed by the limp-wristed role played by the UN in the event, disturbed that the Americans had everything their own way. If *they* are now going to be the world's self-glorifying policeman, I may look back on my pro-Gulf-war stance with dismay.

For the rest, the Palestinians, despite their general suicidal idiocy in every decision they've ever made, must have their own state, and Israel must divest herself of the cancer of occupation. She will certainly have to be pressured into this, though if anyone attacks her I will be on her side. The Middle East must be freed of nuclear armaments. The arms trade in general must be regulated and controlled.

To compare Saddam with Hitler is to exalt Saddam and trivialize Hitler, but both were built up by world capitalism, now dangerously triumphant and rampant. The US in particular, but we too, must realize the harm – political and economic – that unbridled market forces have done and can do, and exercise self control if the 'new world order' is not to be more pregnant with disaster than the old.

Stan Barstow

As with the Falklands, once the aggression had taken place it had to be stopped. But let's not cloak our action in a guise of morality. We armed Saddam Hussein and let him murder his own people. The ones who should be having the restless nights are the diplomats, safe in their beds, who, with both the Argentine and Iraq, failed to give clear signals about where the line was drawn.

There will be no long-term stability until the Palestinian question is settled, and that will call for a better class of statesmanship than we have lately become accustomed to.

11 March 1991

Nina Bawden

I thought the Falklands adventure an embarrassing display of humbuggery: affecting a noble principle, we were in fact behaving like a bully who has found someone small enough to fight. I think the Gulf War is different. Partly our fault, after all: it was we (and the French and the Germans) who sold weapons and poison gas to Saddam in the first place. So it was presumably right to try and prevent further aggression – against Israel, Saudi Arabia. That said, I find it hard to believe that the kind of saturation bombing that kills civilians in shelters and a disorganized army, fleeing with bus loads of hostages, was necessary. The aim, as stated, was to get the Iraqis out of Kuwait. There was no purpose served in turning a retreat into carnage.

9 March 1991

Sybille Bedford

The 'use of Armed Force' – in plain words, war – has rarely failed to generate the next war; and the next. And all war is horrible, in sane terms: death; destruction; the abolition of reasonable, useful, happy pursuits; the sum of loss and suffering well beyond the given harshness of nature and the troubled, fragile condition of man. Armed force, then, organized or spontaneous, is something that many of us have learnt – at last, at last – to feel and think of as inadmissible, obsolete, even criminal. We would choose to cling to the simple imperative: we must not kill, maim, destroy artefacts, do damage to trees, the desert and the sea. This, for me, has been an old-rooted, almost obsessive conviction. At times it wobbles. It remained intact when Hitler invaded the Rhineland in 1936 (oh hindsight); it was shaky when Hitler invaded Poland; by the time the German Army marched down the Champs-Elysées, it had wobbled almost completely (and not in the direction George Bush was recently urged *not* to wobble).

Rightly? Wrongly? All the way to Hiroshima . . . Too late to have stopped the Holocaust.

So in the weeks and days before the Gulf War, I wished – very strongly – against it. I saw it as an unleashing of environmental and human catastrophe (which in fact it was). At the same time I was as acutely aware of the horrors of the Iraqi regime, the ravaging of Kuwait, the threat to Israel, the Middle East, our oil supplies, the risk – quite likely global – of letting Hussein get away with it. I had little faith in sanctions. So when the news of the first sorties came on that January night, it was shock, dissent, as well as relief, even a trace of elation because of what appeared the virtuosity and control of the Allied Command. (*Anything* is more acceptable to the imagination today than the trench warfare of 1914-18.)

At the time of writing, Kuwait has been 'liberated'; our hi-tech stick has been slid into the human anthill of the Gulf. Where now? Look at Kuwait City, look at Baghdad, the Kurds . . . Where there was great misery before, there is vast-scale misery now: more death, more hate, more fear. The oil wells are burning. Saddam Hussein is in place.

So should we *not* have used armed force? Should we *not* have fought this Just War? Before jumping to an answer, one will have to be able to be clear as to what the Gulf War may have done towards preventing some future cataclysmic war. *If* Hussein's nuclear/chemical capability was effectively clipped, that would be a heavy factor in the balance indeed. Another one is that the United Nations has at last been jolted into the role for which it was founded: coming down on aggression, acting to keep the peace. There is also the hope that here and there aspirant aggressors may be deterred. (For how long?)

Recent history has shown that at certain stages of experience people and their countries *can* learn. (I say *country* because anyone who identifies himself with a *nation*, is less apt to think and feel independently.) In Western Europe the spirit of 1914 is dead. (Except for small enclaves.) The possibility of a war between France and Germany has been abrogated in my lifetime. That much – and it is enormous – has been gained. (At huge cost.) In the same time-span the world beyond the West has teemed on with poverty, injustice, rage – often repressively governed, violent and *near*. Too dangerous, too diverse, too angry (the colonial inheritance) for the West to meddle in; too dangerous, too inter-related for the West not to meddle in. The speed of communications has embroiled us all. And there is, and always will be, Trade, the life link with the unacceptable face of expensive arms against cheap fruit and vegetables. So should, and *could*, the Western Powers – with the help, when forthcoming, of the UN – act arbiter, peacebroker, policeman? Nothing was done about Czechoslovakia (twice), nothing about Hungary, Afghanistan; Suez failed; Vietnam is now seen as disastrous; no succour has yet been given to the Palestinians; Hong Kong may be devoured. (Britain managed to snatch back the Falklands.) *Selective* Just Wars.

What cannot be left aside in this context is the nuclear dimension. In most basic terms it is the *threat* of ultimate force in order to deter ultimate catastrophe. To be effective the force has to be sufficiently, that is, overwhelmingly powerful, and it has to be controlled by countries or institutions *adverse* to the use of such force and at the same time *determined*, or appear determined, to use it against a first aggressor. This gruesome equation of terror has worked. Ultimate Catastrophe was held at bay for the last half century. And is not the present slackening of the threat (until proliferation) largely due to that razor's edge determination (yes: Mrs Thatcher; yes: Ronald Reagan) ready for that historical piece of luck, the appearance of Mikhail Gorbachev. These are rough facts to acknowledge for the pacifist, sad facts for any member of the human race; we have *all* come to an appalling pass, we the species that allows itself to over-run the planet, with our hands and developed brain and the genes and lurking instincts of a creature (often brave) struggling for survival. Can the Gulf War be regarded as a move towards Peace and a New Order? Has it staved off worse? Who dares draw the balance sheet – it is a closed mind that can see only one answer to such questions.

2 June 1991

Tony Benn

[In response to the questionnaire, Mr Benn, a former Labour Cabinet Minister and at the time of the Gulf War a back-bench M.P., sent a copy of his speech in the House of Commons debate on the eve of the war. In this debate the Government sought a mandate to send British troops into battle when the deadline expired the following day.]

This is not a debate between pacifists and realists or between those who favour the United Nations and those who do not; it is a debate about how to tackle a very grave problem and a grave attack on international legality.

The House is a representative body. The nation is very deeply divided on the use of force. On 11 December, when we last had a vote on the Adjournment, hon. Members voted by 10 to 1 in favour of the Government for a United Nations resolution bringing us to the point at which force would be used. That very day, Dr Gallup conducted a poll, which has just been published and which showed that only 31 per cent. of the nation believed that force should be used. Earlier this week, *The Daily Telegraph* suggested that less than half the nation favoured the use of force. We in this place must reflect the views of those whom we represent, and that is what I am doing now.

I shall not go in great detail into the consequences of war when it comes; that has already been done. One million men, armed to the teeth – in many cases by the same arms manufacturers – face each other across the Iraqi-Saudi border. The casualties among troops will be heavy. There will be heavy casualties among the people in the region. Nuclear weapons may well be used. As my right hon. Friend the Member for Leeds, East (Mr Healey) said, Kuwait could be destroyed. There could be an ecological disaster if the oil fields are burnt. A worse third-world famine – there is already such a famine – could ensue as developing nations will not be able to pay the high price of oil. The economies of the west, which have depended to a great extent on the finances from the Arab countries in our banking system, could be affected.

War would solve nothing. We are talking not just about the legacy of terrorism, to which reference has been made – although I am sure that there would be such a legacy. The region that would then have to pick itself up would be in a far worse state, even if we scored what is called a victory after what is called a surgical strike, because Iraq and the area around it would have been destroyed.

* * * * *

We have seen – and we will see, when British forces are sent into action – that it is the royal prerogative that allows the Government to go to war. That old feudal anachronism is wheeled out to bypass the House. We note reports in the newspapers to the effect that there will be briefings for Privy Councillors across the Front Benches when war begins. That is the way in which the parliamentary process consolidates knowledge at the top at the expense of others. The Archbishop of Canterbury has been brought forward to bless some 'limited' bloodshed. The censorship of the media has already begun. No journalist in the Gulf is to move beyond his escort officer. The censorship of dissent by the media has also begun. The House is about to see the internment without trial of Iraqis, some of whom may have come here to escape from Saddam Hussein.

We are now experiencing jingoism – a term that I have looked up. I have listened to the Front-Bench spokesman saying, 'We do not want to fight.' They keep saying that. They should finish the poem:

'We don't want to fight, but by jingo if we do, we've got the ships, we've got the men, we've got the money too.'

This country is experiencing the greatest wave of jingoism that I have seen in my life. I am reminded of John Bright's speech in the House just before the Crimean war:

'The angel of death has been abroad throughout the land; you may almost hear the beating of his wings.'

I think that I am the first person who has spoken in this debate who has made any reference to those people in society who actually want war. We know it from the popular press. We see it every day. But nobody has made any reference to it. President Bush said – it was reported in *The Daily Telegraph* – 'We will destroy Iraq.' He said that the Americans would destroy Iraq if Iraq does not withdraw. Where is the United Nations resolution saying that we will destroy Iraq? Hon. Members on both sides of the House have said, 'We must topple Saddam before he gets nuclear weapons.' Where is the UN resolution about toppling Saddam before he gets nuclear weapons? What emerges from debates of this character is that there is a major difference between the UN agenda, which is to restore legality, and the other agenda.

The arms manufacturers have made a lot of profits out of the arms that will be used. Their scientists will be watching to see which weapons work. War sells newspapers and boosts television ratings. It diverts attention from domestic problems.

I am delighted that the French have come out with their initiative because there must be simultaneously an Iraqi withdrawal, United Nations monitoring, an Arab peace force, a peace conference covering Palestine and Cyprus and guarantees of no attack. If the peace initiative put forward by France today were the policy of this Government and of the United Nations, we should avoid war and secure the objectives of the United Nations resolutions. It is no good talking about linkage – a subject that I mentioned when the Prime Minister kindly gave way. We can deny linkage in the conference chamber until we are blue in the face. But the day we attack Iraq and Iraq attacks Israel and Israel responds, the linkage that we deny will be burned into the history books on the battlefield. Then we shall be back where we started. After the war is over, we shall have to come to the French initiative, so why not have it before the bloodshed?

What is our duty to the troops? They are under orders. Our troops have been put under foreign operational command. We represent them in this place; we must question Ministers here. What the Government have done by denying us a substantive motion is to disenfranchise our own troop so that the Members of Parliament who represent them cannot ask the question, and table the amendment, that would allow the interests of our troops to be considered.

This is the most important debate that has taken place in my 40 years in the House. Let my hon. Friends and others be clear: a vote for the Government tonight is a vote for war and will be interpreted as such. Each and every one of us carries a great responsibility. We have to set aside party feelings and electoral considerations, because we must never risk lives to win votes. The lives of millions of people in the world may be influenced by our vote. I beg the House not to give the Government the mandate for war which they want, but to oppose the motion, or to abstain, so that we can look afresh at how this problem might be solved without resorting to the most catastrophic bloodshed.

15 January 1991

[When the House divided, 534 members voted with the Government and 57 against.]

Alan Bennett

I supported the blockade, but not the war. Just as the Falklands War was fought to cover up the failings of British policy in the South Atlantic, so this war came about through US incompetence in the Middle East. Neither the US nor the British governments ever conceded this or admitted it was in part their arms dealing that had made such a war possible. Instead because he had carried the United Nations with him President Bush was able to present the war as a conflict between Good and Evil and not, as it really was, a shameful necessity.

I grew to hate those matey briefings we saw daily on TV with our fearless correspondents too embarrassed or too clubbable to ask the questions that ought to have been asked, sucking up to the generals like sports reporters in the dressing room after a match. I hated General Schwarzkopf's jokes. If jokes there had to be they should have been made against a board detailing the numbers of Our Dead and Their Dead, because that was the real joke, that it was all so easy; rabbits in a sack, fish in a tank, sport.

What the total casualties were has still not been made known, supposedly because they are impossible to calculate. That figure must now include the Kurds, who were Ours at one point, but somehow aren't any more. Though, of course they aren't Theirs either. In this sorry situation, and until the facts of the slaughter are acknowledged, I cannot understand how any victory celebrations (or services of thanksgiving, or whatever name they are camouflaged under) can even be contemplated.

Steven Berkoff

'Sitting in his eighth-floor office overlooking the muddy Tigris River, Naji al-Hadithi, director general of the [Iraqi] Ministry of Information, turned up the volume on his TV set when CNN aired a story about Iraq. Afterward, fingering red worry beads, he boasted to his American visitors that Iraq held a considerable military advantage in the event of war. "During our war with Iran," he explained, "we lost 53,000 men in order to recapture Fao, one small Iraqi town. In the entire Vietnam War, America lost only 50,000. The party that can endure the most sacrifices is the party that will win."' – (*Time*, 21 January 1991)

'Aftermath'

Naji al-Hadithi says, and he must know,
the Director General of the Ministry
of Information informed his yankee friends
or rather boasted drunk with human blood,
'We lost fifty-three thousand brave young men,
to capture Fao, one small Iraqi town,
when we did battle with the Iranian hordes',

as if the sheer multitude of human woe
came from a packet or a slot-machine,
not from my mother's treasures of her womb.
He opened his mouth and made a great dark hole,
'He that endures the biggest pain, the slaughter
on a wholesale scale will be the stronger one.'
He that wades through vats of human blood,
like drunken, demented vampire and numb
to shattered bodies linked to broken brains
and boasts that he can endure the loss, since
he sits in hardened shelter with his boss,
and moves the human toys around the map,
a thousand here and now ten thousand there,
pour oil in water, blood in sand and smile
your drunken glazed-eye grin and gloat,
while million mothers wailing for their boys
sadly cannot share your blissfulness.
So al-Hadithi spends his borrowed limbs
some mothers loaned, no interest payable
and lucky if your equity's returned.
So like a gambler throws good money after bad,
I'll bet a thousand on this town, ten thousand
now on this, he throws the human dice.
Is this some virtue from a school in hell,
to smile at young men's death you cannot feel.
Is it a fault to mourn for every life,
as if each life might be our very son.
He who takes a drunken pride and boasts,
'How many children can you spare today?'
provokes Solomon's wisdom when he said,
'CUT THE DISPUTED BABE IN HALF'.
Al-Hadithi would without doubt be,
false mother who cries, 'Let the baby bleed'.

Isaiah Berlin

I was in favour of armed force.

Unless there are long, very patient, very skilful and painful negotiations between governments, minorities, etc., until at least the rudiments of a possible solution emerge, a general conference could not succeed in arriving at anything like 'lasting peace and stability in the Middle East'.

1 March 1991

Edward Blishen

I'm reminded, and not frivolously, of my days as a schoolteacher. Horrible things would have happened in the playground. Here were boys battered, here was howling hatred, here had been senseless pride, and equally senseless abjection: there'd have been a great complication of old scores being paid off, and new ones contrived: and now would come the inquiry, and rhetoric would be at work. For all that ignobility the most noble language would be found. Playground reality would be left, in no time, far behind. The worst ruffian would turn out to have the smoothest line in remorse or self-justification.

It's bad enough in a school: when the whole world is involved, using increasingly dreadful weaponry, it's not just intolerable – it clearly means that unless something is done, the end for human beings is very near. I can't see that there's any enterprise for us at this end of the century but the desperate effort to find another cure for quarrels than war. Clearly we barely began to do that in the case of the Gulf War. 'Remember, George, this is no time to go wobbly,' said Thatcher to Bush, and she might have been Basher talking to Cosher behind the lavatories in the Stonehill Street playground. I suspect it may be very much a time for being constructively wobbly.

And then . . . how to adjudicate on the question of such a war being right or wrong, when behind it lie questions that must be answered first: the true questions: such as, Is it right or wrong to permit the making and sale of armaments to be an anarchic trade held to be justified if it leads to profit by individuals or nations?

As a conscientious objector in the Second World War, I never felt I had the intellectual grasp (I wasn't sure anyone had) to cover the whole complicated case as to war and peace. I'd been moved to take the position I took then as much as anything by a book of photographs I stumbled upon in a bookshop in the Charing Cross Road, about 1935. They were photographs, hundreds of them, of faces that weren't faces: these were victims of the First World War who'd survived with their faces blown away. I thought then I couldn't be responsible for that sort of thing, and I feel that now. I see the burnt face of the Iraqi soldier in his burnt-out vehicle: I hear the cries of anguish, the voices smooth with victorious satisfaction.

Out of such things I put together a single feeling of revulsion: we have to stop this. We can't go on being wicked, piecemeal: and justifying each fragment of wickedness, and moving on to the next. We have at last, for absolutely practical reasons, to give our complete attention to the entire evil. Either that, or we have to agree that we are a worthless, dispensable species.

8 March 1991

Edward Bond

In the nineteenth century Britain and France took control of the Middle East to protect trade routes to their Far Eastern colonies. The colonies have gone. But the Middle East has become even more important as the major source of oil.

Before they left the Gulf the colonizers fixed the boundaries of the new states to make it easier for their companies to extract and sell oil. In an attempt to keep control they gave the states reactionary governments. In doing this they created divisions among the Arabs. Sparsely populated, fabulously rich countries became neighbours of crowded, desperately poor countries. The West preached democracy but supported dictatorships. The Shah's secret police were also America's secret police. There is no other honest way to put it. America hired torturers to protect its economic wealth. A democracy which corrupts itself in this way cannot understand itself.

The Middle East crisis is part of a world crisis. Technology is exploding in a way which makes the political organization of the whole world obsolete and dangerous. In order to remain in power but still retain the old forms of ownership – and at the same time postpone the socially and politically destabilizing effects of technology – Capitalism must sell, sell, sell. So it needs finance, cheap labour and markets. In return it offers standards of material welfare that in the past were utopian. The effects are felt not only in the Middle East but in the Far East and in Eastern Europe.

Western democracies maintain world power by submitting to the imperatives of the market and technology. Capitalism is enslaved to these imperatives. Decisions are made not to meet human needs but market needs. For Thatcherism they are the same thing. The rich get much richer – but, still, the poor get a little richer. It may be so. But the cultural consequences are disastrous. When both rich and poor are enslaved to technological and economic imperatives, there is no society. And then there is no civilization.

Everything is sacrificed to maintaining the system, but the system has no purpose. It is a dehumanizing monster.

Technology could be a means to creating enlightenment and welfare. But combined with capitalism it dehumanizes us. Our culture is probably the first major culture to dehumanize its people. We live on a cultural heritage from the past but do not renew it. Capitalism could not describe – could not know – its foundations without destroying its justification. It is the most materialist of all cultures but seeks its philosophy in transcendentalism as well as in biological determinism. The results are seen in religion. The Logos becomes the logo and religion is used to express sentimentality and hate. American Christian pop-singers decorate their regalia with crosses and swastikas. What the past used to humanize people becomes a means of dehumanizing them. It is the inevitable logic of capitalism.

The economic system provides goods to relieve social tensions, the political and cultural systems multiply the tensions. The market needs aggression, the politics legitimate it and the culture embodies it in daily practice. Dictatorships claim to use violence so that the community may live in law-and-order. Western governments do not openly use violence – the system creates it lower down in the social structure. Our society terrorizes and represses itself at the same time as it frees itself to enjoy consumerism. The contradiction is at the centre of our life. People suffer more violence in free, Capitalist America than in Ba'athist Iraq – and the violence is culturally and intellectually more degrading because it does not confess its cause. The violence of Americans – and the increasing violence of Europeans – is a product of capitalism. In Western society crime serves the same structural function as the secret police in a dictatorship.

The West has been able to hijack the word 'freedom' because it can deliver 'goods'. Was the Gulf War fought for justice or oil? In the West they are the same thing. American democracy cannot exist without obeying the imperative of the market and technology – its culture and freedom depend on doing so. If the economy failed there would be chaos – and more and more that comes to mean the discipline of some new form of fascism. We have spent vast amounts of money and mind on abolishing the enlightenment, society and socialism – and so on abolishing civilization. Where there is no society there is no civilization – only 'goods' in prosperity and barbarism in crisis.

Large wars – such as Vietnam – destroy the dream of affluence. Small wars – the Falklands, the Gulf – make fewer demands on consumers. They can even be part of consumerism – a sales gimmick or spectator sport. They fit easily into our cultural violence. There were many examples of this in the Gulf. American soldiers talked of 'good guys' and 'bad guys' as if they were in a Western. Killing was sport – 'the captain gave us a pep-talk and then we went out and played'. The leading General bragged like a member of a street gang – he sneered at his opponent for being a military nonentity, yet the campaign is presented as a classic of arms. As the war became more violent the president became more humble, till he sounded embarrassingly like the wise old 'Doc' character in a Disney film. Technology was on our side, our bombs were so smart we could deliver them through the letterbox. (Little boy: 'Don't cry mummy. The nice man screaming overhead says he won't drop his bomb on me . . . only on daddy'.) TV war reports were interrupted by ads for soap powder. And when Iraq offered to withdraw and started to do so the allies went on attacking – ('Some of them went on shooting at us.' Well they would do if you went on shooting at them.) – and so we indulged in one last filthy piece of butchery. The war is said to have restored to America the pride she lost in Vietnam. What sort of people are proud of butchery?

It seems that technology-and-capitalism can give us 'cut-price' wars. But what is the meaning of the nightmare difference between the number of 'their' dead and 'ours'? Perhaps that only long industrialized societies have the discipline and back-up to fight with modern super-weapons. Over the years regimentation has replaced spontaneity, consumerism replaced the search for freedom, want replaced desire. And what does this tell us about the use of nuclear weapons? That the industrialism needed to create them destroys the social means of controlling them and the psychological ability to judge them. To live safely with technology we must become more human – yet the way we live dehumanizes us. That is the chief lesson of the Gulf War.

Today the radio commentator says we must support Hussein in case he is replaced by worse (the commentator means 'Fundamentalism') . . . Kuwaiti fascists shoot Kuwait democrat leaders . . . Western companies scrabble for rebuilding contracts (it is the new name for loot: the logic of Capitalism renames everything) . . . the Emir's palace is to be rebuilt first . . .

I do not excuse the violence of Iraq or our Arab allies. But any politician who says the war has brought peace to Arabia – or even halted a deteriorating situation – is a fool or a liar and probably a looter. But even if it were true, it would be a disaster for us. How can we give justice to others when we are unjust, or peace when our lives are torn by such contradictions? The West is an imprisoned society, but the bars of its prison are invisible – they are its ignorance that it is a prison. Now we have strengthened our self-delusion, buttressed our injustice and added to our confusion. We have fought for the rich against the poor – always a mistake. And we may well have begun the skirmishes of a greater conflict.

11 March 1991

Paul Bowles

I am against the use of armed force in liberating Kuwait, and I do not believe it was used with that purpose in mind.

There is no possibility of peace and stability in the Middle East.

To 'take sides' implies making a choice based on moral judgement. In this instance such a choice is impossible, both 'sides' being equally in the wrong. There is a question: was the exceptionally severe punishment inflicted upon Iraq by the United States and its allies politically expedient? Considering its effect on the countries of the third world, one can only reply in the negative. I think the next war will show us how great a mistake we made.

1 May 1991

Vincent Brome

Post mortems without pathologists are always very difficult. One point remains intact in a welter of contradictions. Commitment to one side or the other too often becomes fanatical. The war in Iraq is not a black and white issue. War is the admission of diplomatic failure but diplomacy for Saddam was simply a delaying tactic. In the event a war conducted for such a cause, with such speed and so few casualties is not a bad alternative. The nature of the cause is complex. Part selfish oil interest, part lofty devotion to international justice. Something had to be done about Saddam and by the luck of the gods and modern technology he has been put in his place. Or has he? The difficulties of peace are worse than those of war.

Recapitulating my first point. It is axiomatic to the liberal viewpoint that fanaticism leads to the Inquisition, the Gestapo and Martin Luther. It is not what views you hold, but *how* you hold them that matters. We are in the middle of a new upsurge of religious intolerance. God preserve us against fanaticism.

2 March 1991

Brigid Brophy

I deplore US imperialism.

10 May 1991

Alan Brownjohn

' "You don't actually deny that you are enjoying yourself, do you?" "No."' – Chris Dunkley (on 'Feedback', BBC Radio 4, 27 January 1991) questioning Brian Redhead about his presentation of war reports on 'News FM'.

The war had its ludicrous features, though not of a kind you could smile at. With nine per cent. Inflation, unemployment cresting two million, record bankruptcies and a huge trade deficit, Britain once again clothed itself in the rhetoric of the past and went to battle. Government hypocrisy, military censorship and media compliance allowed few to reason why without feeling conspicuous and unsporting. If our boys were sent there with the Union Jack to kill unknown foreigners, it had to be right. When our less professional boys took the flag to Heysel Stadium and twenty, instead of two hundred thousand, unknown foreigners died, that was wrong.

I was opposed to the use of armed force, which could not and did not restore peace and lasting stability to the region. British forces went to war not to protect our shores but as the mercenaries of the oil magnates, defending an ugly dictator against an atrocious one. That had to be right too, But the Conservative Government (Carrington, Nott, Biffen, Hurd, Mellor) had been backing the same atrocious dictator for years with guns, butter and embraces. That was not explained. Somehow the Emir of Kuwait was worth fighting and dying for. He was undemocratic, nepotistic, had a murky financial record, three wives, and over forty children. President Ceausescu had all these qualifications except the lechery, but no one fought for *him.*

Old tanks were deployed at London airport, with weaponry likely, had it been used, to slaughter many more tourists than terrorists. Young commentators like Michael Ignatieff deplored the jingoism but backed the bombing: it was unmannerly of knaves like John Pilger to bring slovenly, unhandsome corpses between the wind and their liberal sensibilities. A Labour leader who had been a unilateralist nearly found himself having to back the use of nuclear weapons.

But the Baghdad shelter (where daily-sheltering civilians were not spotted by 'smart' cameras), and the slaughter on the bridges, and the holocaust of the Kuwait-Basra road, were not ludicrous. And our Government and Opposition went along with these calculated atrocities. As a deeply ashamed patriot I want to know why it is Britain goes on and on joining in enterprises like the Gulf War, forever feeding on delusions of power and preening its dead imperial plumage. Why do nice young liberal journalists become evasive when confronted with the patent horrors of war? And how is it that British public figures go on getting themselves into such illogical and unsavoury tangles?

In part, this time, war was an immediate legacy of the Thatcher years. In Washington last autumn, urging George Bush to be a man and promising British subservience, Margaret Thatcher cannot have failed to recall the effect of the Falklands factor on her electoral fortunes. But there are longer-term reasons for this periodic lunacy; and one of them is the fact that the United States invariably approves of it and finds it useful. British delusions are allowed us on licence by the US because Britain agrees (it's called the 'special relationship') to be America's first line of protection in Europe. British military postures are largely dependent on American permission and American favours (like the intelligence vouchsafed us in the Falklands conflict).

In the Gulf, the US, bent on war, set its face against the diplomatic initiatives of Perez de Cuéllar, Mitterand, the Scandinavian countries, Gorbachev, and even a UN appeal by the separatist Soviet republics. Without the drummed-up 'consensus' for the war in Britain and the flavour of respectability lent by British participation, America might not have felt so certain; after all, the Gulf is farther away than Nicaragua, Panama or El Salvador. Loosening the dangerous American connection (though, heaven knows, *not* locking ourselves into a European military superpower of the future) would achieve two desirable objects. It would help to isolate the American military-industrial complex and limit its aggrandisements. And it would render British militarism a little less supportable.

The only genuine chance of a lasting peace in the Middle East would be provided by a permanent conference of nations charged with settling all outstanding problems by every international means short of war. War achieved nothing more than an American vengeance for Vietnam and a boost for Muslim fundamentalism. The problems include tragically minor matters like Iraqi access to the Gulf (comparatively minor, though it was made the immediate reason for war), and huge problems like an agreed policy for oil prices and the establishment of a form of Palestinian autonomy.

I should like to see a freed, non-aligned or less-aligned Britain increasing the chances of such a conference by acting as an honest broker in that process. Is this too imaginative a leap for a Labour Government?

The role played by the British media in delivering a consensus over the Gulf is a different kind of human problem. British self-delusion has a lot to do with the apparatus and the necessities of the media; that is, the tendency of the media to spend money on war and the necessity to justify the cost, Louts behaving typically in tabloids' offices are not so important: a survey during the war showed that approaching forty per cent. of *Sun* and *Star* readers 'did not trust them at all'. But the pleasanter-seeming people in the broadcasting media (generally 'trusted') are a different case.

Two days before the coalition air attacks began, an opinion poll found roughly equal percentages of respondents for and against war. But where did the cherished principle of 'balance' go? On the first day of hostilities Radio 4 cancelled nearly all its programmes in favour of continuous war reporting (sacred exceptions were the morning service and the Archers). It did this without explanation to those tuning in; the television channels adopted similar routines. With the satellites available and many reporters, young and old, out there hoping to make or enhance their reputations by being in on 'the action', it was essential to assume that British people wanted it that way.

After three days of media dedication to war – seventy-two hours of the instinctive war attitudes and, crucially, the war vocabulary passed down from Biggles to Billière, from Alamein to Riyadh, from all the old Dimblebies to all the new – a *Sunday Times* poll registered 5-1 support for military action. Desperate diplomatic moves, large peace demonstrations, appeals by Pope John Paul II were put very low on the news agenda even though there was no uncensored hard news from the front. The airwaves dutifully performed as propaganda media and duly delivered the consensus.

The weight of this open or implicit media endorsement of war carried many decent but morally browbeaten people towards acquiescence in unspeakable and futile horrors. Some of them actually thought they had taken in the moral consequences by *saying* they had. Confronted with the brute facts of slaughter, they were merely managing to dance aside from the truth and take refuge in what governments, generals and airwaves contrived to present as sane, majority opinion.

But I accuse them less than the reporters and journalists who (with a few shining exceptions) became accomplices in censorship and deception, perpetuators of imperial delusion. Corralled by unctuous ministers and unspeakable generals into 'media response teams', regaled with euphemisms and sanitized videos, plied with hand-outs which they sometimes despatched verbatim to their editors, they co-operated to turn it into a virtually *illicit* war. Coalition forces have now removed and concealed the ruined vehicles, the charred emplacements and the incinerated dead in the desert, much as the reporters covered them over with non-language. So thanks to their highly-paid obedience we do not know, may never know, the scale of the savagery inflicted in our name.

And to their everlasting and irreducible shame many of them enjoyed themselves.

26 March 1991

Arthur C. Clarke

Was there any alternative to Saddam and A. Bomb in 1996?

10 April 1991

Richard Condon

If the reasons for going to war have always been cynical reasons, the alleged 'coalition' effort which resulted in the Gulf War is pluperfectly cynical. Declared as necessary to combat aggression, (immediately following the American mission to Panama which sent 25,000 troops to arrest one man who was said to have compromised George Bush) it marched out to the defence of dear little Kuwait, and valiant, threatened Saudi Arabia, calling in such staunch allies as Egypt, whom Mr Bush immediately forgave a $7 billion loan, Turkey who also turned a pretty penny out of the deal, and Israel who was paid handsomely to stay out of Mr Bush's war. To make the world safe for Big Oil, Mr Bush, himself a big oilman, shook down this country and that to pay a fair share of the action, as down payments on the future deliveries of oil. Within weeks of the Iraqi affront, Mr Bush had moved hundreds of thousands of troops and materiel into the Gulf region so that it would be impossible to conceive of having them pack up and go back home in the event that Iraq did accede to all of the 'points' made by the Security Council of the United Nations. Mr Bush 'drew lines in the sand' and cried out that this heinous aggression 'would not stand' while he fed the American people, so discouraged by its politicians, television footage of bombing which was always uncannily accurate and which never seemed to fall upon any civilians, making sure that the international press didn't become 'too aware' of all military action , giving the world instead brilliant personality turns such as 'The Bear', 'Stormin' Norman, and over 900 miles of yellow ribbons to decorate the home front. An 'allowed' 100,000 Iraqis died. Jordan and the Palestinians were ruined. The Persian Gulf was profoundly polluted far into the future. The pall from burning oil wells ravaged the environment of countries as far east as Pakistan and India, but George Bush, at least temporarily, had shifted the American public's mind away from the corruptions of the Reagan administration, the Savings & Loan horrors, the defalcations of the American Congress, the strangling budget deficit, the smothering national debt, the evolving economic recession, and his own slipping popularity. As a stop-gap – temporary because of his fatal ineptitude and dooming political callousness – the entire $50,000,000,000 exercise of the Iraqi war seemed to have been planned to insure his re-election to the American presidency in 1992.

14 March 1991

Maurice Cranston

I think the Gulf War was a just war. In 1935 I believed that war was wrong and that sanctions alone should be used against Mussolini when he invaded Ethiopia. Events proved my judgement wrong. By failing to invoke force against aggression, the League of Nations proved itself a futile agency of peace. The Second World War was the consequence of its failure to mobilize an international military force against the aggressors of the Thirties. I cannot blame the League because at the time I shared the pacifist sentiments which inhibited the use of force.

I believe that Mr Bush's determination to mobilize an international force to thwart Saddam's aggression in the Gulf was largely motivated by memories of the 1930s and of the outcome of the League of Nations' inactivity in the face of the then dictators' invasions of smaller nations' territories. I do not think it should be regarded cynically as a 'war for oil'. The casualties on the Iraqi side were, of course, heart-rending. I do not understand why they did not prompt the Iraqis to rebel against Saddam.

The 'Arab problem', of course, remains unsolved. But it would have been more than a problem if Saddam had been allowed to hold on to his conquest of Kuwait. It would have been a nightmare, for he would undoubtedly have used his control of the Persian Gulf to unleash war against the rest of the world, as and when he chose.

12 May 1991

David Daiches

I was against the war before it started, hoping that Saddam Hussein could be toppled by diplomatic and economic means, but once the war started I wanted a quick and decisive victory for the coalition. Now that this has been won, I am appalled at the cost in human suffering and ecological damage.

And now? The problem of achieving a just and peaceful settlement in the Middle East (and it must be achieved by the Middle Eastern peoples themselves) is formidable. Some land-for-peace (and absolutely secure borders) deal must be worked out between Israel and the Palestinians, but that, difficult enough though it is, is only a part of the problem. I confess to being confused and pessimistic.

26 March 1991

Margaretta D'Arcy

Against. Force only strengthens the Military-Industrial Complex. The beginning of each war carries the seeds of the next one.

It is the women who have been carrying the greatest burden of the war. Women do two-thirds of the world's work, get paid five per cent. of the world's assets, and own one per cent. of the world's wealth. Raising children is not counted or paid as work. But soldiers' killing of those children *is* counted as work, and paid for. Until this situation is reversed, so that women count, and women's work is counted, and the Military-Industrial terrorist Complex dismantled, there can be no peace in the Middle East or anywhere else.

1 March 1991

Jacques Darras

We now seem to have entered a phase of world affairs in which we are re-living, TV-wise, on a diminutive scale, the main stages of all our past European climb to power. To me the first intimation of that oncoming involution was the Falklands – typical nineteenth-century gunboat policy, as the Fashoda clash between the French and the British. Kuwait is of the same order. It had all the ingredients of an *anschluss* down to Saddam

Hussein's Hitler-like moustache and we eager to step in, as should have been the immediate response against the Nazis.

And indeed we were right to intervene even under a delusion. Committing a smaller mistake in order to avoid a greater one will always have the ambiguous excuse of our human fallibility. I must say that I have been impressed by the measured pace of our decisions throughout. Our reluctance to make war long prevailed over any eagerness to the contrary. I cannot accept the negative logic of those, like Noam Chomsky, who take exception to each one of our meticulous steps. In fact, I strongly suspect that many practising sirens have felt frustratingly bereft of their usual gloom. So crushing, indeed, was the end that it had us all reflectively doubt the original legitimacy.

Yet in more respects than one this was a shadow war. That is to say, a war with our own shadows. Let us never forget that we Europeans tailored the map of the Middle East into nations called Iraq and Syria. As for Israel, what a cruel irony that it should have modelled itself on that very European nationalistic pattern out of which came all its European misfortunes! The French Revolution having been the font – the Holy Font! – of nationalism, no wonder that the notion of an *armed nation* should have been the vehicle (an armoured vehicle) through which we French specifically dreamt of secularizing the Middle East, Hence the French-support of Iraq against religion-plagued Iran and consequently the stand of a secular pro-Ba'ath Minister of Defence called Chevènement, in more ways than one the son of the colonial Third Republic.

How are we now to extricate ourselves from so many shadows? By refusing to acknowledge its faulty European origin – that it prefers to dress in legitimate messianic clothes – Israel has become the perfect romantic nation that Germany so disastrously wanted to be. Religion and weapons, what is there to distinguish you from your Teutonic knights? Having myself opted out of my French nationalism to become a nomad on the face of the earth, I feel saddened, taking comfort from the female-orientated New Testament, away from the warlike Koran and Old Testament.

9 May 1991

Michel Deguy

Perhaps the arab nation does exist, but the Arab Nation is an ideal and a war-cry, a Utopia, an agenda, a slogan, a sleeping drug, an amphetamine, a cautery, or an aphrodisiac.

Islam is a religion, but – apart from the fact that there is only one Arab for every five Muslims (M. Rodinson) – the division of humanity into the 'faithful and infidels' is regressive, repressive, intolerable and puerile. Living at a time when Voltaire is unknown on a quarter of the earth's surface gives a sinister twist to Malraux's prophecy: 'the twenty-first century will not come'. There can be no 'Islamic justice': there is only Justice. What we call the West will not capitulate on that. The ideal of law and universality, experience and hope, as seen by a Westerner is stated thus: 'I have to be protected by *your* law (a universal law) against *you*, yourself. 'I' am in the country of other men, strangers and foreigners, and I am always more or less threatened by their particularity, their clannishness, and their 'chauvinism', and I appeal to a law which protects us all, i.e. each one of us wherever we may be against the ethnocentric lynching of a foreigner (which is what I am).

A despot (but that Greek word is too weak) is a man who, because he has the violent power to do it, takes legends literally and makes from their spirit the curse of the death penalty. This is the opposite of that of the artist, the creator of fables, who transforms the letter back into the spirit.

Perhaps we despise the 'Arabs' to such an extent that we consider it tolerable, even necessary, 'for them' to have a totalitarian regime even richer than Stalin's in idolatrous icons of the bloodthirsty tyrant stuck up on hoardings every 100 yards in towns where none of us could live for a week, especially not an educated Muslim with a ticket to New York in his pocket. And I have heard perverted politicians in our Congress murmuring that the *shariah*, since the Arabs 'wanted it' would serve very well to 'clean things up' in the 'Arab world' for the time being, and that it was therefore not worth arguing or fighting to remove from 'them' the illusion that this law could become worldwide.

The Arabs are their own worst enemies. They have done more harm to each other than they have ever inflicted in hatred on the 'others'. No Arab problem, be it Kuwait or Palestine, ever could or should be settled among Arabs. Kuwait and Palestine are not 'Arab problems' but general, international, human problems. Regional issues exist only in relation to global issues, and vice versa.

Oil, which is the source of wealth for a hundred states and of fatal inequality between a hundred partner nations, such as Iraq and Bangladesh or Libya and Mauritania, is not used by the West for the ruin of the Arabs. In the same way, the theme of 'humiliation' is used as an alibi for a propaganda of hatred in ethnic terminology and as an excuse for almost total impotence; the accusations of the unacquittable wrong of the rest throws the veil of 'legitimate defence' over a strategy of hostage-taking and holding to ransom, which flouts international and moral law.

Better to have a corrupt despot, an emir of the gaming tables, but not a destroyer of his people, than an Ashurbanipal without a séance table, taking his authority from a Vision, delivering (by means of forceps forged from the poverty and indoctrination of his people) a mediocre empire hallucinated by the ashes of history and crushed between the two empires of the twentieth century, with the ultimate and visionary aim of 'destroying Israel', a state recognized by the United Nations, protected by the USA and now by the USSR, and used as a haven by Soviet Jews: a dream of blood and grandeur which sleepwalks its way to self-destruction.

The desire 'to be an Arab' is limiting, peculiar, at most a provisional stage opf identification for overcoming even more peculiar local problems and ambitions.

The closure of 'Arabia' to the outside world and the mosques and holy places to infidels can not last long. For one thing, as everyone knows well, it is totally against Western thinking, which is shared by the wider world, which dominates, since it harnesses the resources – a situation which is helped by the tourist economy, meaning the global economy of which the Arabs are, like everyone else, the heirs, beneficiaries and dependants. The twenty-first centuiry will, alas, be cultural or nothing. Everybody will visit *their* holy places, just as for many years 'everybody' has been visiting our holy places. Whether they still remain holy is another matter; it is to be hoped that holiness will remain with us 'to the end of the world' – but in other places and by other means.

In order to move away from its own exclusiveness from the rest, Europe, which used to quench its thirst on the inferiority of the 'others' whose 'otherness' it liked to emphasize, now upholds its abstract plan for universality, for a glittering cosmopolitan concept which it likes to call its culture, i.e. its tolerant scepticism, its spirit of distinction of essences which permits 'real' distinctions between heaven and earth, between powers, between public and private, its project made paradoxical by the 'interpretation' of the 'promises' and achievements, as 'transformations', no doubt, unorthodox, clever, corruptible and which no literal agenda could complete; an anthropomorphosis carried on by the metamorphosis of the same transcendentals or spiritual motives (the good, the true, the beautiful . . .).

Our racism against the Arabs gives those who feel humiliated the alibi of their 'humiliation' and seems to justify this hatred 'such as there has never been', this religious hatred. The evil of capitalism, the sale of arms in particular, throws harsh light on the radical harm done by savage liberalism, a 'state of culture' more Hobbesian than the state of nature.

The impotence of the UN, the bias towards Israel, the incredible arrogance of the American ethos, the air-conditioned nightmare of wealth, all provide alibis and delusions of the presumed innocence of 'the Arab'. The distancing of law from violence prevents us from demanding retribution, gives the dictator the advantage of an outlaw; he makes himself the Prosopopeia of his god, the personifier of the impersonal.

Saddam, quite unaware of the ventriloquy of the modern age which makes him condemn himself out of his own mouth, ignorant of the paradox which dispossesses by possessing him, Americanises him, and which only an outsider could see (the way of the Westerner changing from one 'world' to the other?), talks of Islam as a cultural organizer, reproaching the English-speaking novelist for having disfigured 'the face of Islam' in the great trade-off of brand images.

If the absolute still haunts this world, it is in the form of absolute contradiction. America's god (in God we trust) is not God. He is the god of the religion of good citizenship.

Can one distinguish between the USA and America, make a distinction between Americanness and American man? One must be able to, both in order to explain the fascination which leads half the human race to want American citizenship at the very time when there burns in the same people a hatred of the USA, and to understand how the same French intellectual waiting to return to a US university can keep saying that he detests American culture, and to demand whether a general, workable sharing is possible between the best of Democracy and the worst of liberalism.

Is *homo americanus* viable? No. Not one of his precepts could apply abroad, even if certain ones of them were incontrovertibly universal. What television viewers across the world fail to see is that the success of the American couple, unearthly, appalling, polluting, destructive and autistic as it is, depends on its taking seriously, by way of half-hidden compensation and principle of reality, American good citizenship, the American 'religion' of law and order. Now the USA is a democracy; Israel is also a democracy. The West, as we call it, will not budge on that point.

How could the USA be changed? A strange question . . . This strange question expresses everything that is right in the criticism of the US by those who can see what it can't see for itself. A 'moral' person is one who is ready to accept that others are right about where he is going wrong, his own personal injustice, and accepts that conversion would be a good idea; 'good' depends on conversion (*metanoia*). But how could a nation be a moral person?

A nation is an entity which cannot be reduced to subjectivity, even if one, as a subject, uses the words of moral responsibility to make it speak. On what conditions can a people (a mass, as Canetti would say) of 'subjects' make itself subject, make itself be *like* a subject, i.e. convert itself to wisdom, reason, to what Solzenitsin calls autolimitation, which would be limitation to the self. Within what limits is this vigilant 'limitation' (that is to say, expertise in pretence) thinkable or sensible?

The change to be brought about, which we, who belong to the Empire would wish to obtain from the USA, from America, which would affect their manner of being, in other words their being itself, not their trade, nor their quotas, will not be made by enormous conflicts in which they represent the best (the 'good' in American language), what is best for *us* (democracy, etc.) and from which they emerge as victors, with a power that 'proves' them right.

This 'being' would not have to be simply an 'image'. I count myself among the most sceptical scrutineers of Americanness. I think I can judge the power of contagion of Americanness like this: it is when the model apes itself that the spread of its image is most virulent. This cultural state is maintained mostly by the secession of intellectuals who distinguish themselves from vulgarity to the point of not recognizing their nationality, or even their second nature which we are reproached for slandering and which we are thought ridiculous to malign.

But what makes a national entity? Is there an attribute, or a *vinculum essentiale* which might in some way be modifiable; how can one change a way of being?

The Islamic world, westernized for and by the power of reason, for and by the ideology brought by scientific and technical modernity, and yet medieval in its religion, its clericalism, its theocratic hierarchy and ideology, more torn than any western nation ever was by its gulf between rich and poor, lords and servants, the mighty and the servile, men and women, sledge-hammers and sound-guides, this world will not overcome its internal division, its schizophrenia, by a 'world war', by the dream of a world-wide Islamic republic, by the 'destruction of Israel', or of the entire Western world.

Better the hypocritical but self-critical regime of international law trying by the management of the United Nations to 'institute a new world order'; better to have the struggle, the contention which is basic to western thinking, between the legal red tape and the reality of injustice, an ever too vacuous desire for world peace and the immoral scheming of self-interest! And if the law is made for the jurisprudence of pleas, some spiteful, others peace-seeking, and to be betrayed, ridiculed or misunderstood, it must nonetheless try to impose its humane transcendence, so that the ignoble pleas, the false preferences and the confusions can be denounced as such, be assessed and rejected as such, by firmly, consciously and remediably keeping the formal and the real separate from laws which are either too weak or too repressive, and from violence.

From where have these resourceful international relief organizations, Amnesty, Médecins sans frontières, Ecologie, sprung in recent years, if not from the extremity of the injustice inflicted on people and on the earth by enemies who are not demonic, hostile powers, but thoroughly determined agents of horror and destruction, and as though by touching the unimaginable limit of evil, the sense of good is invented by negation, by way of righting the wrong, the sum total of the law as that of 'you will not do that'.

Saddam Hussein, the recently promoted scourge of God (Allah Akbar) – starts his wars in his own time and varies his style: by way of internal genocide he gasses his Kurds, and joins the exclusive club of which Pol Pot is President; against Iran, using an interest-free grant of dollars, he bought himself a more classic war (Ba'ath *versus* Imams), in the style of the First World War (trenches, artillery and tanks); with Kuwait it was annexation in a single night, Anschluss-style; for Israel, scudded in the back, he decided on an assassination attempt in the style of the hired killer who has signed a contract. Against the Coalition he launched into, and lost, a sophisticated catastrophe, allowing them a scenario of realistic manoeuvres for the Third World War. Things which international conscience and the rules of warfare strictly proscribe, he considers his right – ubiquitous terrorism, general hostage-taking and holding to ransom. And we have allowed him, without making a declaration of war and making a madman's use of the rhetoric of Arab hospitality, to take hostage thousands of western citizens while thousands of his fellow Muslims and poor enslaved Asians could not even aspire to such a status.

Like village idiots who fail to mention that *their* act of aggression or accusation came first, — or like an over-confident French pedestrian taking protection behind his right of absolute priority, he, like all dictators, makes 'legitimate defence' his priority, by making out that the infinite sequence of war started with the aggression of the *other party* – '*they* started it.'

For there to be peace, one day, there must be a sharing of 'the same', — Jerusalem,* for example, must be owned and be shared by several; it is a problem of single or multiple ownership, of the involvement of several rather than one.

How can we put an end to the system of appropriation of the unique, personnified subject and its attribution; and to the sharing by juxtaposition (which is precisely the ruse of the wrong answer in the Judgement of Solomon)? It is a problem of symbolism, of joint possession, of space. Are we all equally far from the spirit of a solution? The Arabs are at least as far away as we are, since they still believe that it will be a question of the triumph of *the* Arab nation and the return of *the* religion to the City . . .

France no longer belongs to the French; it must be shared out in a totally new way.

*'*Bene aedificata cujus participatio ejus in idipsum.*'

Anita Desai

Armed force was not used to prevent Tibet from being invaded, nor Afghanistan. Why was it used to protect the Emirate of Kuwait? Because it could afford to pay an army of mercenaries drawn from 28 nations, or because those nations needed a war to rescue them from an economic recession and to revive the armaments industry which had suffered a blow with the end of the Cold War, by the totally disproportionate and savage bombing of a small, poor country, its civilians and even its retreating army? Certainly no other reason is apparent, and both are disgraceful.

Since the UN has been revealed to be in the keep of the most powerful (rich and well-armed) countries of the West, the only hope for peace in the Middle East is a debate in which all the nations involved (including Israel) participate, without interference from those to whom one can no longer look for just and humane leadership.

8 April 1991

Margaret Drabble

I was against the use of armed force in liberating Kuwait, and in favour of giving sanctions and diplomatic pressure time to work. The fact that some of the foreseen disasters have not occurred – massive allied casualties, a prolonged ground war, unprecedented ecological destruction, the use of chemical or nuclear weapons – balances my response, as does our knowledge of the violent and oppressive nature of Saddam Hussein's regime, long available to the West through such impartial observers as Amnesty

International. Like everyone else I am glad the war was short and, on our side, relatively bloodless, though one cannot feel 'comfortable' (to use a military term) about the overkill produced by the wealthiest nations on earth bombing the hell out of one of the poorest.

I cannot share the optimism of those who believe that a Pax America will bring lasting peace to the Middle East. They do not even believe it themselves, or they would not be so terrified of catching American or British airlines. This war has disastrous implications for the Third World, for Arab-Western understanding, for world security. The Americans will be fortified in their belief that they have a right and duty to arrange the affairs of other nations as best suits them (I heard Dick Cheney say that the Americans would get rid of King Hussein of Jordan if only they could find an acceptable alternative — acceptable to *whom*, eh?) and their leaders seem to have little sense of how this makes them not loved but loathed by the Wretched of the Earth. Film of captured Iraqis kissing the hands of American liberators is not going to make life more peaceful over the next decade. Nor will Victory Parades cheered on by those who have done nothing more dangerous in the war effort than watch CNN. Lasting peace and stability will come only when America realizes that Arab conflicts require Arab solutions, policed not by the USA but by United Nations troops. And Palestinian claims must be considered in any settlement. If they are not, surely by now we all know the consequences?

6 March 1991

Gavin Ewart

First, let me say that I very much agree with W. H. Auden, that a writer in this sort of context is no different from any other citizen. His or her opinion (though we would hope it might be an intelligent one) is no more valuable for being that of a 'writer'.

I was in favour of the use of armed force, as a last resort, in the liberation of Kuwait – as long as this was according to the communal will of the United Nations. How successful sanctions might have been, if continued with, we shall now never know. Supporting the UN is of the greatest importance, since it is the only international tribunal.

It is very important that a superpower, like the United States, should not be allowed to pick and choose which Resolutions it supports with action, and which it doesn't.

The Americans have invaded Grenada, a British possession, attacked Panama, and done nothing about the Israeli expansion in Palestine. This amounts, in general, to an 'America First' policy.

Lasting peace and stability in the Middle East are going to be a long time coming. Russia should be involved (a common frontier). Triumphalism of the Thatcher kind ('Rejoice!') must be avoided. Bush is not too bad (Reagan was an idiot, and Vice-President Quayle still is one).

6 March 1991

Ruth Fainlight

Your questionnaire arrived a few days after hostilities were halted and before the official cease-fire, when armed force seems to have liberated Kuwait and opened the way for radical changes in Iraq. As at the time of the Falklands conflict, I find myself unable to deny or accept the power of armed force to alter circumstance – and deeply unhappy in that realization. The arming of Saddam Hussein and the encouragement of his regime made it inevitable that he would use those arms in an attempt to extend his field of operations. As long as the uncontrolled manufacture and sale of arms continues, I do not see how lasting peace and stability can be restored to the Middle East or anywhere else that conflict might arise.

5 March 1991

When you first asked me to write about my responses to the Gulf War, the Allied military action was still taking place and, in spite of profound reservations, I hoped something good might come of it. Now I understand that what I mistook for Reality was in fact a demonstration of *realpolitik* which has surpassed even the most pessimistic or cynical predictions. With each passing day I become more aware, with a sour and shameful consciousness, of how I – like almost everyone else – was diverted and manipulated. The 1976 Pike Report to the House of Representatives' Select Committee on Intelligence, (still suppressed), details the same betrayal of the Kurds to Saddam Hussein that is happening now. The political freedoms (comparative but real) of the West cannot be allowed to them – nor to the Kuwaiti or Iraqi opposition – if to do so would threaten the control over the area and its oil reserves on which the West's continued enjoyment of those freedoms ultimately depends. And so the linkage between indifference and self-interest continues.

10 May 1991

Daniel Farson

> 'Any man's *death* diminishes *me,* because I am involved in *Mankind*; and therefore never send to know for whom the bell tolls; It tolls for *thee.*'
> – John Donne

It had to be done, and it was done well. From a tactical point of view, it was one of the most successful campaigns in history, even though there was little to push against towards the end. Every commander needs luck, and many of the President's cards were dealt in his favour, but he played them skilfully, with impressive single-mindedness throughout.

Every reason therefore to be thankful; less so to rejoice. There is talk as I write this of a Victory Parade, but that might be tempting fate. Throughout the war the Americans were simplistic, and this could have been an advantage in the short-term. It allowed the arrogance of regarding Iraqi life as of lesser value than our own. Generals gave us appalling figures of the saturation bombing, and did so nonchalently as if they were dealing with units rather than men. When the war was over, the casualties proved astonishingly low – for *us* – justifying the Blitzkrieg – but the casualties for *them* were estimated at around a hundred thousand. Not just the loss of young men, but the loss to their families, and the effect on their children which will linger for the rest of their lives. Also, the wretched aftermath for the animals: sea birds drowned in oil; the hippopotami starved to death in the Kuwaiti zoo. All of this was the obscenity of war, yet the only *sadness* I heard – apart from the understandable anger – came from the Falklands hero, Simon Weston, who expressed compassion for the enemy. He had a soldier's understanding, reflecting Wellington's comment which may be a cliché but is no less true – 'the next greatest misfortune to losing a battle is to gain such a victory as this'. In the midst of glory, it was unfashionable to ask for whom the bell tolls.

The other fallibility which will rise to haunt us, was the lack of understanding, or even the wish to understand the Arabian and Islamic mentality, with all the subtleties of saving face, and the deviousness of their politics. Evidently, it did not occur to us that once we toppled Saddam we might have the appalling legacy of a Shi'ite regime, with the risk that Iran would be encouraged to gnaw at the secular foundations in Turkey, laid down by Ataturk, with new determination. We may have been justified in using armed force; to expect a lasting peace and stability would indicate that we have learnt nothing of the problems and horrors to come. And yet . . . as they say . . . and yet, if President Bush *can* achieve a compromise peace between Israel and the Palestinians, restoring their role in the Middle East, that would be a victory indeed. Personally, I cannot be certain of anything.

8 March 1991

Howard Fast

There is an old and very wise saying, as follows: 'He who saves a single life saves the universe, and he who destroys a single life, destroys the universe.' It takes some thinking about, and it's worth copying out and looking at now and then. I quote it because in all the wild celebration of victory, the gleeful satisfaction of TV speakers and interviewers, the resonant pronouncements of anchormen, there is hardly a mention of compassion, pity or regret for anyone who did not wear the uniform of the United States. Even the dead and wounded of the French, British, Egyptians, Saudis and Kuwaitis were brushed aside and mentioned only in passing. And for the 80,000 Iraqis who met their deaths in the man-made hellfire that we created in the desert, and for the 100,000 more who were injured, arms and legs blown off, testicles shattered, stomachs torn open – for them hardly more than a demographic snort of satisfaction.

We propose to believe in God. We say there is one God, and this is the creator of all things, and men and women are the children of God. In fact the act of going to war, the act of being a soldier in motion explodes the God thing in a million prayers, pleas, fears, and crying out to the same God, help me, save me, bring back my child, my son, bring back my son who is your son, who is on his way to kill as many of your other sons as possible, and let him kill as many of your sons as necessary to bring him back to me, safe and sound and whole.

Are we all crazy? Think about it.

The newest paladin is, of course, General Norman Schwartzkopf. 'Stormin' Norman, as Barbara Bush told us on TV, grinning her delight in the great victory. Certain obscene things were done in Kuwait to Kuwaiti citizens captured by Iraqi soldiers, and as General Schwartzkopf put it: 'Men who do such things are not human, they are not a part of the human race.'

That's a very comforting thought, because when you take away a person's humanity, you remove him from the human race, and then, of course, killing him become an easy act indeed.

But hold on – the General was talking about Iraqi torture, and of course in the heat of things, he forgot about the men we sent to Argentina and to Bolivia and to El Salvador to teach the police of those nations the art of torture, and he certainly cannot be blamed for not mentioning, in the flush of his victory, that indulgence in torture is not a racial characteristic or a national characteristic or a religious characteristic.

I'm not putting down the general. War is his business and profession, and at that profession he is better than anyone else. At the same time, righteousness is the lifeblood of slaughter, the rationalization of slaughter, and the satisfaction of slaughter. Every one of the 80,000 Iraqis we put to death – and don't even mention that it was a fair fight, the most technologically advanced nation on earth, population 240,000,000, against a backward non-industrial desert nation of 17,000,000 – every one of those Iraqis who died was a man of flesh and blood, each with dreams, with mother and father, with brother and sister, with son and daughter, with all the power to love that we possess and with all sense of pain that we possess.

And they brought it on themselves? What nonsense, and yet I hear it everywhere, they brought it on themselves. When all the voices for peace and sanctions raised here in the United States could not deter Mr Bush from the course he had chosen for his own ego satisfaction, do you imagine for a moment that the protest of some poor Iraqi peasant could have deterred Hussein from the course he had chosen. These 80,000 human beings we have slain in the sands of a desert more than ten thousand miles from our shores bear no guilt; they are not the bad guys; they are people, plain people, simple people, poorly informed, deluded by their leaders as we in the West are also deluded by our leaders – indeed as plain people and poor people have been deluded by their leaders since history began.

Is anyone, in print or by voice on that electronic network which covers our nation, going to say that we have done a terrible thing, a thing that defies all reason and sensibility, that we have massacred a nation, that given the choice between peace and war, we chose war? Or are we going to celebrate the slaughter with victory parades and a thousand miles of yellow ribbon. If we have lost, not 80,000 but only a few hundred, it is not numbers but the useless death of boys hardly more than children – our own. Yet in a way, they are all our own.

A man who was nailed to a cross two thousand years ago, by Roman soldiers, said of his killers, 'Forgive them, oh God, for they know what they do.' That's all that's left to us, a plea for forgiveness.

12 March 1991

Lawrence Ferlinghetti

As of 1 May 1991, Kuwait has not been 'liberated' (as your question seems to envision).

America has instead returned Kuwait to the medieval custody of its royal dictators, which was the primary US purpose of the whole despicable operation. As soon as it was accomplished, President Bush went fishing. The oily frontiers of empire had again been secured, and let a million Kurds curdle. Corporate fascism rules again.

Leslie Fiedler

The causes of all wars are ambiguous; the allies side by side with whom we fight them are dubious; the results are uncertain. Nonetheless, certain wars against unambiguous forces of evil or repression (like Saddam Hussein) must be fought. Our history reminds us that not rational negotiations but brutal armed conflict destroyed the power of Hitler, ended slavery and indeed assured our independence to begin with.

Such wars of course must not only be fought, but (like the War in the Gulf) unequivocally won. There is no such thing as a good lost war, nor for that matter, a good lost peace; and winning the peace will be – as we are ever more painfully aware – much harder.

6 May 1991

Penelope Fitzgerald

I'm opposed to the use of armed force, and that if it's employed in support of business interests then I'd prefer that to be stated frankly which on this occasion, of course, it wasn't; as far as Britain is concerned, I think it fair to say that we went to the help of our allies with not much hope of making anything out of it (but what are allies, exactly?). If the higher, or moral ground is going to be taken, I don't see why we should go to the help of Kuwait, but not of Tibet.

I believe that peace in the Middle East must come not from its political but from its religious history. The three deeply interconnected faiths all have the same salutation – the prayer or invocation for peace. I believe that could stand for something if the Middle East experts could be silenced for a while, because if these are not Holy Lands, they are nothing.

30 March 1991

John Fowles

Having to liberate Kuwait as we did seems like performing a complex brain operation with flint knives. There was a savage discord between what seemed necessary and what might have been, given intelligence and foresight, possible. All our technology was in the wrong field – how to kill and starve, not how to prevent and save. I'd put almost all the blame, on both sides, on the desperate lust and greed for personal profit that bedevils our wretched species. All lasting peace is a pipedream for as long as we let that dominate us.

5 May 1991

Mark Frankland

1. For: the intervention was an unfortunate necessity.
2. By painful, mutual compromise.

1 May 1991

John Kenneth Galbraith

I favoured the application of sanctions and embargos on Saddam Hussein. I opposed the initiation of military action and went twice to Washington to make clear my position before the Congress. I take account not alone of victory in war but of people who must face the terrible prospect of death on both sides and then the dismemberment and death. And from long observation and experience I'm conscious of the political and social uncertainty but certain tragedy in the aftermath.

8 May 1991

John Gittings

Saddam Hussein took Kuwait hostage on 2 August 1990, and threatened to pull the pin on the people of Iraq as well as of Kuwait if the police tried to storm his position. It is always excruciatingly difficult to deal with hijackers or hostage-takers, but most people agree that the best way is to use persuasion and diplomacy. That way was the route of economic sanctions plus negotiations. The US pushed sanctions for a time, but never negotiations.

Once the midterm elections in early November were over, President Bush made clear what had been intended all along: Sanctions would not be given time to work. Saddam would be ousted by force unless he committed the psychological impossibility of total public capitulation. Saddam did respond by releasing the western hostages – which could have begun the dialogue. Others – the French, the Russians, Edward Heath, Willi Brandt – thought there was room for a diplomatic settlement. The massive US build-up and refusal to negotiate never gave us a chance to find out if they were right or wrong. In the last days before the ground war, after Iraq had been pounded mercilessly from the air, we did find out that Saddam was not after all contemplating national suicide. He openly accepted the previously unacceptable: to get out of Kuwait. His frightened conscript soldiers – most of them no more than civilians in uniform – were not allowed to do so. Tens of thousands were slaughtered needlessly in the ground war which Mr Bush persisted in launching.

The West had previously acquiesced in Saddam's war against Iran and made only token protest at his human rights abuses. This is not irrelevant history but a reminder that we share some of his guilt. To bomb the people of Iraq was to punish them twice over. It was certainly not the route towards restoring 'lasting peace and stability'. If Saddam now falls Mr Bush will claim further justification. We cannot be in the business of Reckoning a grotesque balance sheet – would more, or fewer have died under his regime than perished in the war? We should point to the hypocrisy of ousting one dictator when he turns awkward, while allowing a dozen more to flourish around the world. The lesson of the Gulf War for the dictators and feudal rulers of the Middle East (including Syria's President Assad) is certainly not to choose democracy and peace. It is that if hi-tech weapons are so wonderful, we want them too. And in the case of the Gulf states that security can be secured by hiring mercenaries with the proceeds of oil. There is no incentive here to reform the Arab state system or tackle the injustice of Palestine. Mr Bush is proud of vanquishing the Vietnam syndrome by the application of 'overwhelming force', but he has not reckoned the long-term cost.

28 March 1991

Robert Greacen

For moral and practical reasons I oppose the use of violence in the conduct of human affairs. Therefore I opposed the use of armed force in the alleged 'liberation' of Kuwait. This does not imply that I condoned the invasion of Kuwait by Iraq or the crimes of the Saddam Hussein regime. Crimes have most likely been committed by the Allies of which we have heard little or nothing.

I believe that Aldous Huxley's words in 1937 in reference to the Spanish Civil War still hold good: 'The choice is between militarism and pacifism. To me, the necessity of pacifism seems absolutely clear.'

Lasting – or even temporary – peace can only be restored to the Middle East by prolonged dialogue between the parties directly involved. Such dialogue ought to be supported by generous aid, moral and material, by the rich countries of the world. To be realistic, however, there seems little chance of this happening.

6 June 1991

Hugh Hanning

To the complex issue of Kuwait I brought a couple of unwavering prejudices: those of World Order, and the new supremacy of the missile.

On the first, I cannot be faulted, since Cecil and Jean [Woolf] had kindly published a book of mine on the subject just two years earlier. Its theme, which was rather novel at the time, was that thanks to a change of heart in Moscow we could now construct the United Nations as its founders always intended, and that the West should remember what it has been trying to do for 40 years and take Yes for an answer. This was Bush's strategy and was surely right. The only codicil is that we must stick to it and not allow ourselves to be pestered by international lawyers.

The supremacy of the missile was the theme of a report I was privileged to write five years earlier for a group headed by Marshal of the RAF Lord Cameron. All agreed that the 'platform' – ship, aircraft, tank – is not what it was, certainly not as cost-effective as the corresponding missile. In the event, it was the air-to-ground and ground-to-ground missile which enabled the coalition to win with hardly a land casualty.

But I do not pretend to have 'told you so'. The Pentagon expected 10,000 casualties, and one gave them credit for information which outsiders did not have. On this account I wanted to 'give diplomacy a chance'. I still believe this was not done. We found ourselves almost 'fighting for a conjunction': we would hold a Palestine conference after Kuwait, but not as a result of it. *Post* but not *Propter*. Like many better men, including half the US Senate, I would not have gone to war until this diplomatic knot had been disentangled. But in the name of World Order, I supported the right to do so.

Perhaps my main insight is still valid and still ignored. This is the theorem that it is crazy to go to war without having first warned the aggressor. That lesson we have learnt in NATO, where it works – but nowhere else. Failure to warn the aggressor was the cause of both World Wars, the Korean War, possibly the Vietnam War and certainly the Falklands. Since it often happens in July or August I call it the Goodwood Syndrome, to convey a vision of policy-makers playing truant at a race meeting when the avoidance of a major war depends on their success in warning the aggressor that he cannot win. At the time (1988) I wondered whether I might be over-doing it, because surely we had learnt that lesson after the Falklands. But not a bit of it. Two years later it happened again, in Kuwait – bang in the middle of the Goodwood season. Saddam joined the company of the Kaiser, Hitler, Kim Il-Sun and Galtieri.

The US Congress is holding a post-mortem on the subject, to find out who was to blame. We should do the same. But one way or another, for the sake of those who died, could we please kindly *not do it again*?

8 April 1991

Jacquetta Hawkes

Though a founder member of CND in the late fifties, I have never been a pacifist. I was a supporter of the Falklands War and so was interested to read the excerpts from authors' letters on the subject. None of them showed any consideration at all for the Falkland islanders themselves. I suppose, as some words from A.J. Ayer suggest, that these writers all feared that support for a population of British origin would amount to showing 'the ugly face of jingoism'.

When the issue of using force against the Iraqi invaders arose I thought about it as long and as seriously as I was capable of doing. Against it was a normal horror of warfare, the probability that technological advance would increase the violence and, as days went by, the obvious fact that President Bush had always intended to fight. There was also the prevalent assumption that the Americans would make a mess of it again. But in favour of war was the unbounded evil of President Saddam Hussein, the cruelty he had inflicted on the Kuwaitis and the near certainty that he would have to be stopped sometime. What finally decided me in favour of force was, however, a positive good: the hitherto unimaginable unity secured within the UN and the vast increase in its authority that success would bring. I also came to recognize that this was not likely to be a long war. Over before 2 March was my lucky and recorded guess.

5 March 1991

John Heath-Stubbs

We should have used force against Saddam Hussein, as an international criminal, in 1988, when he used poison gas against the Kurds. There is no particular moral reason for liberating 'Kuwait', to which Iraq seems to have quite a good claim. A Middle East conference should be called to settle all problems of the area including the Israel-Palestine problem.

11 March 1991

Thomas Hinde

Well – yes, I was in favour of force to free Kuwait. I know most of the arguments against: a neo-colonial war, oil the true motive, total inconsistency with our response to similar events elsewhere, especially the Iraq invasion of Iran. But the fact that you have made mistakes was no reason for not doing one thing which on balance seemed right.

We are all victims of what we see and hear, and draw conclusions from too little evidence. The BBC Horizon (or was it Panorama?) programme on Saddam Hussein finally convinced me that he was a monster, for whom there was nothing to be said.

The future of the Middle East – that's too big a subject. Would it be fair to think that it is going through its Thirty-Years-War phase? If so the solution would be a single state, like greater Germany. But that took 200 years.

March 1991

Michael Holroyd

I might have supported armed intervention in Kuwait by a genuine United Nations force. But I am generally opposed to military interference by any country in the business of other countries – in the long run it so often provokes more trouble. Every country needs to make its own mistakes, commit its own crimes and undergo the painful evolution of its own history, rather than have what may seem higher standards imposed on it by foreign cultures. People have compared Saddam Hussein with Hitler, and perhaps rightly so. Had there been no Versailles Treaty in 1919 there would have been no Hitler in 1939. Had there been no 'pragmatic' political interference by Britain, the United States and others in the Middle East between the two world wars there might well have been no Gulf War this year.

There is no security with dangerous creatures like human beings. But the best chance of peace in the Gulf will now (28 February) depend on the rapid retreat of all troops back home, and a foreign policy of unusual tact and understanding from the United States. This must include a rejection of 'market forces' in the sale of arms abroad. But if special deals have already been done with Israel and Syria, it may not be easy.

28 February 1991

Elizabeth Jane Howard

Hitler dominated my youth, and the idea of a dictator with an aggressive war machine recurring has been not only a nightmare, but in some cases a reality. Interference with any dictator's aims, while it may seem desirable, turns out usually to be impossible, since at least half of their aggression is directed towards peoples within the country they rule, and democratic powers don't seem to have had any successful answers to that. We got rid of Hitler at enormous expense, and helped Stalin (whose record for murdering people within his country – over 15 million — was twice as bad as Hitler's) to increase his power. We did nothing whatever to aid Tibet when the Chinese – utterly unprovoked – invaded it, and Tibetans have suffered and continue to suffer to this day. We might, I suppose, take the pragmatic view that people like Hitler, Stalin and Saddam Hussein *do* have a charisma that gets them to where they are or were, that this is rare, and that assassination of them might at least rock the regime, and give the people a chance to change their political situation.

I, in common with most people, thought that the Gulf War was a very dangerous enterprise, but I did think that getting the Iraqis out of Kuwait would entail the end of Hussein. What has happened seems to me the worst of both worlds. For more Kurds than Kuwaitis are now dying and existing without hope of any future that could be said to be either secure or promising. A 'safe' camp – and if I were a Kurd I'd be pretty unsure about that – may be better than a death camp, but they never asked to be in a camp at all in the first place. Camps are no way for human beings to live – look at the

Palestinians. Meanwhile, the colossal amount of money that the war has cost would probably have made a life-saving difference to the millions facing famine in Africa.

The situation in the Middle East will never, I think, be resolved until and unless the western powers go a long way to freeing themselves from their dependence upon oil. It is difficult to believe now that the motive for getting Hussein out of Kuwait was simply moral indignation, or surely the uprising against him would have been backed by the US, etc.

The only hope seems to me that the United Nations can somehow negotiate territory for the Palestinians – thousands of whom must also feel hopeless without a future in *their* camps, and for this, the Western powers must have no axe to grind and the other Arabian countries would have to be involved in giving them some territory instead of castigating Israel as the country solely responsible for the problem. Arab solidarity needs to consist of more than agreeing to hate the Israelis. But given that with the exception of Israel, all Arab countries are dominated by men, I feel that any lasting peace is a long way off. Women and children don't want wars, but neither of these vast categories of people have any voice. But I also feel that those of us who have the good fortune to live in a democracy have not yet accepted that a lower standard of living may well be the price we should pay for peace in the Middle East.

11 May 1991

Hammond Innes

The Falklands, now the Gulf, two wars within a decade in which our involvement was a matter of principle, not self-interest. The first is still a drain on our resources, and the Gulf was certainly not fought to safeguard our oil supplies!

So why? Shades of the Pax Britannica?

I know the waters of the Gulf and the desert south to the Liwa; Sheik Zaid himself showed me the Buraimi Oasis in the days when the United Arab Emirates was the Trucial Oman and I was researching *The Doomed Oasis*. Even then, before Saddam Hussein and the Ba'athis took over, the Iraqi soldiery I saw in Baghdad looked scruffy and dangerous, a race apart from the bedou of the Rub'al Khali.

Somebody has to stop the psychopathic bullies of this world. Logistics make it impossible to fight them all, but sometimes somebody has to stand alone, as we did in 1940. Nobody wants to die, but whatever the risk, I am glad to belong to a people who are prepared at times to face consummate evil when it is loosed on the world. Freedom is not for ever, not a gift from God.

5 March 1991

Robert Irwin

Saddam Hussein headed a fairly secular and, in some respects, progressive regime, which was genuinely committed to anti-imperialism, pan-Arabism and the liberation of Palestine.

In Saddam's mind at least, the occupation of Kuwait was linked to the liberation of Palestine, for Iraq's annexation of Kuwait was certainly intended as a prelude to the occupation of the rest of the rich and corrupt Gulf Sheikdoms as well as of Saudi Arabia. In the long run, an expanded and enriched Iraq might indeed have been able to take on Israel militarily, while using economic power to keep the United States at bay. With only a little more time and a lot more oil wealth, Iraq could certainly have produced both nuclear weapons and the means of delivering them. (It should be noted that, in Iraqi Ba'ath party thinking, the liberation of Palestine does not mean merely the establishment of an autonomous Palestinian regime in the West Bank and Gaza Strip: it means the total destruction of Israel.)

Iraq's frontiers were drawn up by British imperialists in the aftermath of the First World War. Though the country does not have natural frontiers, it does have ideological ones. The ideological frontiers have been drawn by Ba'ath party ideologists, from the 1940s onwards, most notably by Michel Aflaq. In Ba'ath thinking (which has been strongly influenced by the writings and deeds of Hitler and Stalin) there should be no separate nations called 'Iraq', or 'Kuwait', or 'Syria', but only one Arab nation which would extend from the Atlantic to the Gulf (and include the Iranian province of Khuzistan, which Iraq prefers to call Arabistan). All Arabs must be one and, since this unity cannot be achieved by consensus, it will have to be achieved by violence. Michel Aflaq and his pupil Saddam Hussein have demanded struggle and sacrifice. According to Aflaq, 'in this struggle we retain our love for all. When we are cruel to others, we know that our cruelty is in order to bring them back to their true selves, of which they are ignorant. Their potential will, which has not been clarified yet, is with us, even when their swords are drawn against us'. One must love not only the end, but the means to the end. It is this sort of 'love' which has underwritten the Iraqi regime's reliance on show-trials, public hangings, acid vats and gouged-out eyeballs.

Since this 'love', which recognizes no frontiers, has set vast armies on the move, the Gulf War was a necessary war and necessarily a horrible one. Its outcome, the triumph of the United States and its allies, will have few good consequences. However, the consequences of the Allies not fighting that war would have been worse yet. I cannot imagine how future peace and stability in the Near East will be achieved. The rhetoric about a 'New World Order' is just that. We will be very lucky indeed if we get back to much the same mess as before.

11 March 1991

Roy Jenkins

[In response to our questionnaire, the late Lord Jenkins of Hillhead, one-time Labour Home Secretary, founder of the Social Democratic Party and biographer, sent us a copy of his speech made in House of Lords debate on the Gulf Crisis, 17 December 1990. The following text is taken from that speech.]

It is just over three and a half months since we last debated the issue [of the Gulf] on 6th September. The Government then received very strong support from all sides of the House and not least from these Liberal Democrat Benches. I ventured then to say that the crucial and challenging part of the enterprise was to accomplish and maintain the marriage of United States power with United Nations moral authority. If that could be done, there was a prospect that the issue could be resolved without conflict; and that if this, alas, did not prove possible, then it would be more like the Korean war, although, hopefully, less drawn out and less bloody than the Vietnam war.

The essential differences between the two were that with regard to Korea the United States had United Nations support. In respect of Vietnam, it did not. In Korea the war was essentially a success in the sense that it achieved – although at great price – the major objective. In Vietnam no success was achieved.

I still believe that that parallel has validity. However, one of my perhaps unspoken assumptions in September has turned out to be almost exactly the reverse of the truth. I thought then that the difficult part of the operation would be to keep the sustained moral support of the United Nations. The near unanimous resolution of early August, I feared, might be difficult to repeat. The military power of the United States, and its willingness to commit it, was, I thought, a more assured thing. If anything, I – and I believe a good number of others – believed that there might be a danger of the United States acting too bellicosely on its own, perhaps supported only by Britain.

In my view that is hardly the position today. First, the United Nations has turned out to be much more steadfast than I had expected. Just over two weeks ago I visited New York for four or five days to give a lecture to an organization operating under the auspices of the United Nations and almost under the shadow of the United Nations building. By a singular feat of mistiming, I managed to arrange my lecture to coincide within 10 minutes with the key vote in the Security Council. There were less ambassadors present than had been expected but they were better occupied with other matters at that time. The result of the vote was undoubtedly highly satisfactory. It could be argued that the terms of the resolution were a little loose, but nonetheless it embraced every necessary action.

However, in contrast with the greater than expected steadfastness of the UN, during that week in the United States I gained the impression that the United States was not at the present time a nation poised for action and, if necessary, for sacrifice. The President, who certainly cannot be faulted on his desire for peace, will have to devote just as much attention to leading his own public opinion inside as well as outside the armed forces as he has paid to cosseting the marginal members of the Security Council.

Despite that somewhat disturbing lack of a concentrated national will in America, I nonetheless believe as strongly as ever that the issue has to be seen through to a successful conclusion. There is nothing discreditable about trying to achieve that conclusion by diplomatic means. That was indeed specifically envisaged in the third part of the governing Security Council resolution of 2nd August. But the satisfactory conclusion has to be achieved and there is precious little sign at the moment of a promising negotiating framework. Therefore the possibility, putting it at its lowest, of having to do so through military action looms closer. Obviously, it is not a pleasant prospect but the very fact that the United Nations support has been so successfully mobilized makes it all the more difficult to dodge. If, having mobilized such an international front against Saddam Hussein, he nonetheless gets away with it, the consequences for any authority in the world will be devastating.

If that were the outcome it would never again be possible to mount a major United Nations action to deal with a world crisis in the way that has been done during the past three to four months. Without doubt the reaction of the Security Council to a crisis would become a matter largely of indifference. The devastating position – a word which I use with care – would be that both the United Nations and the United States would be fallen idols. In other words, both the idealistic and the *realpolitik* theories of world authority would come crashing down together and the post cold war world could be an even more dangerous place than when the two superpowers could at least take the strain against each other in a predictable way.

The paradox of the world today is that, while America has emerged as the clearly victorious superpower, the other having been forced to desert the field, she has done so as a somewhat exhausted victor. We in this country have been through that experience and ought to be sensitive to it. Neither the strength of the US economy nor the psychology of her people leaves her fitted to discharge the world leadership role which she brilliantly and responsibly carried out during the zenith of the American imperial age from 1947 to 1965. It is probable that she would now like to hand on that baton of leadership as we did to America during the second quarter of this century. But the fact is that there is nobody to whom she can hand it on. That is the paradox of the world today.

The relatively large dynamic economies of the world at the end of the century – that is, Germany and Japan – have powerful muscular bodies but reclusive temperaments. Perhaps that is natural and desirable in view of their history, but it is a fact. As I have previously said in his House, I do not share the view that Germany is a potential and dangerous juggernaut. I agree with the comment made by President Bush in Baden-Würtemberg four weeks ago; he said that he would like to see Germany play a greater not a lesser part in world affairs. Nonetheless, there is a danger that we shall enter the post cold war world without many sinews of world authority and without much sureness of world leadership. If we can resolve this crisis satisfactorily we shall minimize that problem; if we fail to do so we shall vastly maximize it.

Ludovic Kennedy

Now that the Gulf War appears to be over, I must say how tired I became of those whining Willies who showed up on radio and television every day to say we should have given Saddam Hussein more of a chance. There was a Jesuit Father on the *Today* programme saying that war was so dreadful, we should do everything to avoid it. His was the attitude that nearly did us in during the Thirties when Hitler was rampant. If we had had the guts to fight him when he marched into the Rhineland, we might have been spared the Second World War.

There was every indication that Saddam's vast army was created not only to conquer Kuwait but Saudi Arabia and Syria too, to make him undisputed leader of a new Arabian empire stretching from the Gulf to the Mediterranean. That we have stopped him has been due entirely to the strength and resolution of the United Nations; and, for the first time, that is a wonderful augury for the future.

23 March 1991

Frank Kermode

'If it were done when 'tis done, then 'twere well
It were done quickly . . .'

Well, it *was* done quickly, but, as we have seen, and as many voices warned us, it is not done. It is perhaps true than even those voices, so certain that there would be slaughter and destruction, did not prophecy the flight of the Kurds and Shias, though the failure of the coalition to help their insurrection might not have greatly surprised the prophets.

I cannot claim to have been certain about the rights and wrongs of armed intervention, only that if it came to that the suppression of Saddam and his party seemed to me the paramount war aim; the restoration of political integrity to Kuwait was important but in a sense incidental to our proper purpose, and anyway, as the voices also warned, it could only be achieved at the cost of wrecking the country.

In view of our part in the creation of Iraq, and our ensuring that the whole area was politically combustible, we have a clear responsibility to control the damage. Among much else this could require the exaction of concessions from Israel. I have been a frequent visitor to Jerusalem and think I have some understanding of the thoughts and moods of intelligent Israelis. History tells them, with horrible emphasis, that to give up anything is to risk giving up everything. They could easily have lost the Yom Kippur War; the Syrians descended from the Golan Heights (which Israel would now be asked to yield to the enemy); they might have taken Galilee on the first day of the assault, and the rest soon after; and another holocaust could have ensued. Hence their intransigence, which seems, even to the liberal minded, a necessary posture, however much they may disapprove of the Lebanon adventure and of fanatical fundamentalist territorial claims. They might conceivably be prepared to make concessions if their reduced territory could be infallibly secured. But such a guarantee would probably waken again the prophetic voices; it could in the end lead to more wars, more agonized mass migrations, more displays of self-interest, more betrayals, And even those who are prepared to think about that prospect – by no means everybody, for to many, the frightened as well as the fanatic, it is unthinkable – find themselves close to despair.

26 April 1991

Maxine Hong Kingston

This war has been strange, wrong, fast. And my writing, which I dedicate to peace, is slow. I have been working on a Book of Peace, trying to imagine peace and to invent a language of peace. It may take me a decade to complete. The war broke into the book, which is only about 100 pages along. Here are pages 71 and 72:

I'm hearing the warplanes again roaring day and night whenever I think to listen. The nightmares have come back – B52s covering the sky wingtip to wingtip going somewhere to carpetbomb it, and there are missiles, rockets, giant maces, and other flying weapons of my own imagination – all moving at uniform speed and having to fall sooner or later on populations. The roaring woke me up this morning; I looked out the window at the actual sky, and saw darting between clouds a silver airplane, an equilateral triangle, like a spear head, definitely a warplane, a bomber. Just as I was about to turn away, I saw another such plane come through the clouds. They were going west, the direction the planes in my dreams usually go, which must be the route to Saudi Arabia. Then a flock of ducks flapped by, then a single white bird, then a passenger plane, a long white cylinder. I wonder what a C-6 Transport looks like, one of those flying gasoline stations – big as a football field. A young friend tells me he runs laps and rides bikes inside his plane after delivering the tanks.

The fleets of killer planes were hallucinations that first appeared during World War II, when I was born. As a child, I was afraid of the planes coming to get me, but now, my horror is that they belong to my government, and they are constantly going from my country to do harm on my behalf. Another war, and again I'm on the side with the most weapons, and the most ghastly weapons, and again we're the invader, killing children and chasing an enemy fleeing on bare feet. I am ashamed to be an American, I am ashamed to be a human being. It was during war that Virginia Woolf wrote her Book of Peace, *Three Guineas*, then drowned herself. She could not bear the roaring in her mind and the roaring in the air ('Duncan saw an air battle over

Charleston – a silver pencil and a puff of smoke'), But she did leave us with the story of the village woman who refused to roll bandages and knit socks for the troops. The thought that there was such a woman heartens me, and I won't kill myself. Though I am almost wiped out, timid and estranged – 90% are in favour of this war, and they feel 'euphoria', according to the President, at the war from the air, and more euphoria at the invasion on the ground. They are primitive; if we're winning, they're for it, and whoever kills the most wins. If they are praying any decent prayers, I cannot hear them through the roaring.

19 April 1991

Timothy Leary

The Political Goals of the American invasion of the Holy Land:

1. To re-elect the president. Saddam Hussein sent 500,000 young soldiers risking their lives in the dangerous desert for the glory of the Leader. So did George Bush order 500,000 American youth to risk their lives to re-elect him and to distract attention from his mismanagement of domestic affairs.
2. To strengthen the control of the Republican Party.

The Military Goals of the American invasion of the Holy Land:

1. To restore the prestige of the militarists which has suffered since Vietnam.
2. To use the $2.7 trillion worth of war toys built by the Reagan-Bush regimes.

The Economic Goals of the American invasion of the Holy Land:

1. To bail out the oil companies.
2. To bail out the weapons industry. Even Democratic politicians fight to profit the defence industries in their areas.
3. To distract the attention of the public from the collapse of the American economy during the Reagan-Bush years.

The Religious Goals of the American Invasion of the Holy Land:

1. Onward Christian Soldiers: to continue the Crusade against the heretic Islamic heretic devils.
2. Apocalypse Now! To fulfil the prophecies in the Fundamentalist Bible; to trigger off the long-awaited Armageddon-Jihad Holy War.

The Racist Goals of the American invasion of the Holy Land:

1. To indulge the favourite pastime of white, middle-class American males; to use high technology weapons to kill third world civilians and coloured people.
2. To assemble an American army of half a million ground soldiers, poor, uneducated, disproportionately black youth to act as hand laborers (at low pay), to act as servants for the officer-class which operates/manages the high-technology from safe, comfortable places.

Peter Levi

I never thought well of Saddam Hussein, but I did wonder whether he might have an arguable case against the sovereignty of Kuwait: but then I had always regarded the Gulf Emirates as a ramshackle and shameful construction, and was surprised it had not collapsed already. I now know that Hussein neither had nor felt the need for any arguable case. It is clear that he manipulates a very wicked regime, and deserves to be obliterated.

But war? An American war? I suspected (and I now eat my suspicions) that the Americans could even lose a war of this kind. I hated the idea of such a war, but I could never, at any stage, find an alternative, or any serious argument against war. Knowing what I now know, I wish only that it had all been much quicker, though I see that legality had to be preserved and so time lost.

The stable peace of that region of the world is not a good subject for generalizations. No doubt the possibility of compromise may emerge. I like the Kurds very much at the moment, and have done for thirty years, but they have been losers in my lifetime. I do not foresee any stable peace, for the indefinite future; it would entail revolutionary changes of heart in Iran, Iraq, Turkey, Syria, and most of North Africa.

12 March 1991

Ira Levin

If a gang of marauders invaded the house on the corner, wouldn't you call the police? And if the marauders declined to negotiate and were pillaging the house and maltreating its occupants, wouldn't you expect the police to move in?

Lasting peace and stability can only be restored to the Middle East by wiping out its present inhabitants and resettling the land with Chinese. Since no one likes that concept – except perhaps the folks who gave us Tienenman Square – the next best plan is to do exactly what the coalition forces did, remind uncivilized zealots of all stripes that the UN is real and means business.

21 March 1991

Robert Jay Lifton

War is exciting, especially when you win. And America is now in the full flush of triumph. But was this really a 'war'? And what did we lose in 'winning'?

Our ostentatious embrace of victory – our triumphalism – poses grave problems for the state of our national soul. Our claim to glory can hardly erase, psychologically or morally, some highly unpalatable features of our behaviour in the Gulf.

Just about all of the fighting there was done by our side. To be sure, the Iraqis positioned a large army in Kuwait, and they killed people with Scud missiles, fired mostly at civilian targets. But they could never mount any real opposition to our overwhelming technology of destruction. Concerning our air offensive, a taxi driver summed things up accurately enough in declaring to me: 'This ain't no war. It's just us dropping bombs and killing people.' Nor does aiming at military targets make that any less true.

The ground war turned out to be not very different. It consisted mainly of our tanks moving rapidly through Kuwait and Iraq, the only real impediment to the advance that of arranging custody for the enormous number of enemy soldiers seeking to surrender themselves to our forces. Here and there Iraqis did some fighting, but hardly enough to permit them to qualify as participants in a 'war'.

This does not mean that American troops were not in danger or that they, as individuals, behaved badly. But what our policies brought about was the devastation of a small, industrially backward, third world country – the annihilation of much of its military forces, the killing of many civilians, and the destruction of the life-sustaining services of its major cities.

What epitomizes this war more than anything else was our mass killing from the air of fleeing Iraqi soldiers. With our cluster bombs, as one pilot put it, 'We hit the jackpot'. And according to another, the slaughter accomplished by waves of fighter-bombers attacking a vast column of fleeing Iraqi soldiers estimated to be 20 to 30 miles long, was such that 'it was close to Armageddon'.

We cannot long postpone the questions we are now avoiding: is this responsible behaviour on the part of a country claiming to be a humane democracy? Could we not have avoided much of the slaughter by ending the war much earlier, as the Soviets and many others wished us to do, while still achieving the goals laid down by the United Nations? Could we not have avoided war altogether by pressing sanctions and a diplomacy of common security?

The still more difficult question is what our actions in the war have done to us as a people, We became quickly dominated by an ugly pattern of war psychology that justified the killing of large numbers of defenceless people. Our high-tech weapons eased the process by enabling us to remain numbed to and dissociated from it. The same war psychology required us to view our soldiers as noble heroes toward whom opposition to the war would represent betrayal.

What then emerged was an aggressive patriotism – not the kind that celebrates love of one's people and homeland but the more narrow and nasty kind that Samuel Johnson once called 'the last refuge of a scoundrel'. It led not only to idolatrous flag-waving but to policies of hounding, threatening, and ultimately ostracizing those who failed to do so – as in the case of the basketball player who declined to have a flag sewed on to his uniform because he was an Italian Christian pacifist.

How much racism was evoked is hard to say. We did not attack the Iraqis because they were non-whites (we had non-white allies in the war) but iut is hard to be sure that our willingness to destroy on such a large scale was not influenced by that racial difference. Certainly many in the Middle East have that view: 'The Arabs are not human in American eyes, They step on us like we are ants,' was the comment made by a Jordanian shop owner.

Also of great importance is a psychological tendency we may call military high-techism, a relationship to our advanced military equipment that enables us to view our own individual lives as more valuable than those of people without such technology. That pattern can become lastingly enshrined in a form of high-tech nationalism. We then run the risk of seeing ourselves not only as a blessed country but as the agent of an all-powerful technological deity. Militarized high technology becomes equated with absolute virtue, and as possessors of that virtue we have the duty to be the most powerful of world policemen. American militarized nationalism reached a troubling crescendo during the President's address to both Houses of Congress when (as the *New York Times* reported) he 'basked in the atmosphere of triumph, which produced cheers at his every mention of the military'.

We are capable of much better. Large numbers of Americans have had grave misgivings about our war in the Gulf, and many who supported it are likely to join in a national reassessment of what has been involved. Can we not re-connect with the wave of universalism that has characterized the late twentieth-century rebellions against oppressive regimes in Europe, China, and South Africa? But to do that we need first to confront our own experience in the Gulf not so much in terms of what we have won as of what we have lost and must regain.

1 March 1991

David Lodge

Writing this some time after the end of the Gulf War, I am struck by how much harder than usual it is to be wise after the event. In January I was in favour of using sanctions rather than armed force to liberate Kuwait, for two reasons: (1) it seemed to me that Iraq, with its one-crop economy, would be peculiarly vulnerable to sanctions, and that it would be a great step for mankind if the United Nations were able to bring a delinquent member state to heel by non-violent means; (2) it didn't seem to me that British interests were sufficiently threatened to justify putting the lives of British servicemen and women at grave risk.

In the event our casualties were extremely light; and since Saddam Hussein has so far survived a devastating military defeat it seems unlikely that he would have been toppled by the effect of sanctions. To that extent I, and those who thought similarly, seem to have been proved wrong. On the other hand, the war has brought hideous suffering and death to hundreds of thousands of innocent people, who otherwise would have been unaffected or at least subjected to a more tolerable level of misery, and has caused horrendous ecological damage. One must be glad that the illegal annexation of Kuwait has been reversed, but I don't see how anyone with access to a television set could feel confident that the cost of the ware in human suffering was proportionate to what was achieved by it. The only thing that seems certain is that, like the Falklands War, the Gulf War was caused by diplomatic failure (by Britain in the first case, by America in the second) to send clear warning signals to a trigger-happy totalitarian government. I have no new peace-plan for the Middle East to put forward, but I am sure we need better diplomacy to avoid future conflicts.

15 May 1991

Edward Lucie-Smith

The United Nations intervention in the Gulf took place at a time of widely recognized ideological collapse. The ideological elements which played so large a role in the attitudes of intellectuals towards the Spanish Civil War and, later, the Vietnam War, hardly counted for much here.

The only convincing reason for non-intervention would have been total pacifism: that is, the conviction that making war is wrong at any time, in any circumstances.

The reasons for intervention were twofold – belief in international law, and *realpolitik*.

The notion of international law goes back to the Middle Ages and is deeply rooted in western culture. If it has any meaning, it leads one to the conclusion that it is surely not right for one sovereign state to devour another – certainly not on the flimsy grounds given by Saddam Hussein for the invasion of Kuwait.

In terms of *realpolitik* it was more sensible for the oil-dependent west to check Saddam Hussein's ambitions immediately, rather than waiting for him to invade Saudi Arabia.

The war demonstrated the immense technological superiority of western armies and armaments, and the shortsightedness and lack of will of western statesmen. Since Saddam Hussein supplied the obvious motivating force of Iraqi expansionism, the aim should have been to get rid of him completely. By stopping halfway to this objective, the United States and its allies triggered off not one but two civil wars in Iraq and made sure that the conflict would have no decisive end.

The opportunity was lost to obtain a full settlement in the Middle East, which would have had to include a full settlement of the Palestinian question (itself largely a product of earlier indecisiveness on the part of western statesmen). Instead the West is now entangled with a second, equally intractable problem – that of the Kurds. The parallel between the situation of the Kurds and that of the Palestinians is to me striking.

5 May 1991

Peter Luke

I'm delighted to be asked to answer your questionnaire because it may help to clear up my own woolly thinking on the subject. After listening to all the radio pundits I usually found myself at the end of the day agreeing with the last person to speak – which shows that I am either admirably open-minded, or that I have no mind of my own. But, no, I do think that the execution of Operation Desert Storm was the right and necessary thing to do and I do not think that the fact that I am an old 'Desert (Western) Rat' conditioned my thinking in that respect – at least, not much.

Now the job has been effectively done we can perhaps see better where everybody stands. Saddam Hussein was crafty to play the Palestinian card and King Hussein was unfortunate in being forced to play the Saddam one. Despite Israeli intransigence, bolstered by the American Jewish vote, the Palestinian issue must be solved and, in all fairness, why not the Kurdish one too? The only man strong enough, rich enough, and popular enough to do what is necessary is President Bush – if he can find a velvet glove big enough to conceal his iron fist. Having witnessed the thoroughly nasty time had by all in the Gulf, perhaps the Lebanese and Syrians may now be more inclined to be reasonable and give everybody back their hostages.

As an afterthought, my answers to the question *vis-à-vis* the Spanish Civil War, Vietnam, and the Falklands would have been very different and quite inconsistent with the above.

12 March 1991

Roger McGough

1. I am against the use of military force in liberating Kuwait. Never more so than when witnessing the ease with which the coalition forces crushed the Iraqis.

To undertake military action of such magnitude and at such cost when millions of people are dying for want of food is unjust and immoral.

2. Perhaps, when a kind of Middle Eastern Common Market is set up to share the wealth of the region more evenly, to control its defence policy, and to promote democracy and religious tolerance.

17 March 1991

Armistead Maupin

I was disgusted by the whole sorry spectacle from beginning to end – from the so-called 'initial euphoria' of the bombing to the sight of Americans cheering for instruments of death in the streets of Washington. It wasn't a war this time; it was a mini-series called Desert Storm, so slick and prepackaged that even the kids could stay up and watch. Two hundred thousand killed? A country incinerated and an ocean polluted? We sure as hell didn't see it on television. Having learned from 'the lesson of Vietnam', the oil-owned American press performed its task with surgical precision, shielding our too-sensitive eyes from the gore, manufacturing just the right villains and heroes, blaming those Iraqi civilian deaths on – who else? – the civilians themselves. No wonder it was such a 'clean' operation; we insisted on our right not to know.

13 June 1991

Stanley Middleton

I was in favour of a further trial of sanctions rather than the use of armed force.

The differences in wealth, culture, beliefs and fears, as well as the importance we attach to oil, make peace in Middle East countries almost impossible We must try to reach stability through the United Nations by constant consultation and by agreed arms limitation. It would be a tragedy if the richer Gulf nations, impressed by the success of US military technology, began to expand their own arsenals.

There is a great opportunity for the United States to give a lead here, if only they will take it.

5 March 1991

Spike Milligan

Very simply this war was necessary. Saddam Hussein runs parallel with Adolf Hitler. If ever there was a just war this one was. The great tragedy is, by reason of international law, the man is still allowed to be at the head of his country with the same dubious scheming mind.

7 May 1991

Adrian Mitchell

I am opposed to the killing of human beings in any cause whatsoever. As Blake knew and the Buddha knew and Gandhi knew: everything that lives is Holy. Wars lead only to more wars.

Lasting peace and stability in the Middle East and in the world will remain a mirage until the nations abandon their pride and greed for love and understanding. For everything that lives is Holy.

10 March 1991

Naomi Mitchison

I was against the military 'liberation' of Kuwait. No doubt casualties of the armed forces of America, Britain and a few other allies were admirably small, but the death of both enemy soldiers and civilians in and after the taking of Kuwait City has been large though so far uncounted. It all depends on who you are talking about whether the deaths are of those you know about, or strangers, perhaps from other cultures, and other religions. I think that other possibilities of dealing with the Iraqi government should have been tried vigorously before it came to war, and to the painful things which have happened, not only to those directly in the war but to countries such as Jordan which are caught between two loyalties.

2 March 1991

Sveva Casati Modignani

How can one be a convinced pacifist and at the same time consider the liberation of Kuwait by force to be right? It would seem to be a contradiction, however it is one that becomes clearer when what one had anticipated to be a long and bloody war turns out to be a short, though painful, contained conflict. Can we, as non-violent people, condone the use of violence? It is possible. The case of Mahatma Gandhi is perhaps significant. Gandhi believed that if a man was raping his daughter he would be a coward if he failed to intervene. It seems to me that the action taken by Saddam Hussein against Kuwait is analogous to that of the rapist and that he should be dealt with in a similar way.

Peace and stability in the Middle East must begin not just with a resolution of the Palestinian problem but of the Muslim dream of revenge. Any such resolution must obviously take into account the political and economic interests which revolve around the great *jihad* for oil.

Tariq Modood

Iraq had legitimate grievances against Kuwait but they did not justify an invasion; moreover, its military and demographic superiority over its neighbours on the Arab side of the Gulf were enough for it to achieve a lasting regional dominance without military aggression if Saddam had a modicum of the political skills that we expect in those who aspire to rule. The invasion of Kuwait was therefore an inexcusable blunder and Saudi Arabia had a right to ask the Americans and others to come in to guarantee its security. UN sanctions and an American military presence should have been used as a basis to strengthen, not undermine, the search for an Arab diplomatic solution. It was unforgivable, however, for the Saudis (were they given a choice?) to allow an American military build-up which could only lead to an Arab humiliation of one sort or another.

I cannot reconcile myself to the liberation of Kuwait by the destruction of Iraq. Not just for humanitarian reasons, nor for the racism it is fostering (American pilots enjoying their 'turkey-shoots'; attacks on Muslims in Western Europe), but above all because this war of a few weeks was a major set-back in a much bigger war – the long war for Palestine. Rightly or wrongly, the battle for Palestine is seen by Muslims the world over as the test of whether the long decline of Muslim power can be reversed: if Muslims can uphold the rights of the Palestinians they may yet once again become a world force, if they cannot uphold those rights they will continue to be all puff and no substance – suitable material for American 'turkey-shoots'.

Peace in the region would require comprehensive, especially nuclear, disarmament. But how can this be achieved when Israel will not participate and no one who has the power to make her do so will use it? In *Leviathan* Thomas Hobbes wrote: 'the fear of death is the beginning of politics', Like much of Hobbes's state of nature this is most apt in international affairs. Israel can, if at all, be dragged to the negotiating table only by coming to know and fear the alternative. Peace in the region can only begin the day after Israel suffers a serious but not mortal defeat in battle. By then the feudal lords of the Gulf will be permanent exiles in Mayfair.

22 March 1991

Dervla Murphy

The weapons were sophisticated, the emotions primitive. The resulting violence marked what may one day be seen as a watershed in human history.

Although the Gulf conflict ('war' seems inappropriate) was limited in time and space, it has rubbed relevant noses in a sticky question. What happens next, if men continue to invent and sell increasingly 'efficient' weapons, while neglecting to devise equally efficient political methods for the control of human aggression?

In Ireland the complex Gulf Debate got stuck in a predictable rut. Too few questioned American propaganda/misinformation and those who did, and who opposed the use of force, were labelled 'Lefties' (ugh!). The much larger pro-Allies faction seemed unaware of the existence – in Ireland as elsewhere – of a considerable number of non-Lefties who for decades have abhorred the ruthless duplicity of American foreign policy, the alarming ineptitude of American diplomacy and the unrestrained brutality of American militarism.

To totally destroy one country, in the process of 'liberating' another (i.e. returning it to the rule of corrupt autocrats) is not only a moral outrage but an offence against common sense. For twenty years Iraq's 'Ba'athist regime has been among the most viciously repressive in the world, with the Iraqis themselves as its main victims. Now millions of innocent Iraqis have been made to suffer still more, without even the consolation of Saddam's overthrow. In our inter-related world, all the citizens of those democracies who funded and armed Saddam, despite his appalling crimes against his own people being common knowledge, must take a share of the blame for the annexation of Kuwait and its terrible consequences. We allowed our governments to get away with tacitly supporting tyranny until suddenly it impinged on an inconvenient (for us) area. And then we failed to protest against the American abuse of UN mechanisms to justify the American determination (evident from early August) to 'smash Saddam's military machine'.

16 March 1991

Robert Nye

1. For.
2. I have no opinions. We might pray for peace, perhaps.

John Osborne

I've given up 'taking sides' long ago. However, I always thought it was idiotic going through the whole charade and masquerade of acting under the 'control' of the United Nations – a bunch of corrupt despots and criminals without any moral or practical authority whatever. The Americans and British should have ignored them, gone on to chuck out Saddam Hussein, restore order stable enough for an irresolute, feeble and recidivist UN to take over and gratify the sanctimony of those who 'support' it.

1 May 1991

Frances Partridge

I am entirely against the Gulf War, as I was the Second European War and those in Vietnam and the Falkland Islands. Moreover I remember the start of the First World War, and had reached a position of complete Pacifism at 16 (in 1916). War breeds war and force force. The only things that could possibly create Peace are reasonable discussion or persuasion. Or as a last resort assassination of the key aggressor, just as a high-jacker is killed to save innocent passengers. Before the Gulf War the USA and allies had been steadily selling arms to the Middle East countries. Then with vastly superior strength we have pounded them into submission, leaving behind civil war with all its horrors, horrifying desolation, lack of basic needs like water and the threat of epidemics. Now the Kuwaitis are beginning to inflict what they have suffered on their neighbours, civilians included.

The rules of war are a mockery.

The only way to lasting Peace in the Middle East or anywhere else in the world is *total disarmament*, since as we produce more and more sophisticated weapons men become more and more savage and elaborate in their cruelty. I see very little hope for peace in the future, and if we do not disarm we will certainly blow the world up in the end.

Edward Pearce

The war was wrong because it rested upon a false chivalry, the rescue of a little state from invasion, and a false political sensibility, objection to Saddam's tyranny. The US has suported, sustained and undertaken invasions of sovereign territory: Nicaragua, East Timor, Panama. It has cherished and credit-rolled a litany of tyrants: the Greek Colonels, Hugo Banzer, Marcos, Duvalier, Somoza, Pinochet. At the very moment the bombing of Baghdad started the US extended new credit to the d'Aubuisson regime in El Salvador, the one with the death squads.

The war was odious in Britain because intelligent judgement was overwhelmed by a sluice-tide of tabloid nationalism, because the chief opposition party lost either its nerve or its discernment in a rush to conform and was joined in this by parts of the educated press. At the *Independent* and the *Observer* unintelligent pro-Americanism and power worship got the better of independent thought. The clash between Robert Fisk's reports in the *Independent* and that paper's pitiful leaders illustrates a general failure.

The war was an evil because it allowed the British to treat battle as therapy, a substitute for all the economic success we don't have, something which led to extensive bad mouthing of the Germans for their doubts and reservations. The British sounded like nationalists, gourmands of war and like people with a slenderly veiled malice towards more successful neighbours. Soldiering used to be the profession of ne'er-do-wells. This is not true of individuals given the professional competence of the army. But for nations it may have become the case. We behave like a country with nothing to lose by the distraction of war in which, as is not true of commerce and manufacturing, we exhibit a talent.

The Americans used the war, the British needed the war. But at the end of it we were counting dead Arabs and not minding. For war has upon nations some of the effects of murder upon individuals. We distance guilt from ourselves, we deny the value or humanity of those we kill. We snuggle into the alibi of military necessity.

The perception that killing 100,000 men mostly conscripts or inducing cholera by bombing water supplies might be wrong is denied to us. The stupid people surrender themselves to the red mist of patriotism, and most of the clever people set about rationalizing the deeds done in that mist. To fight such a war is to take a long step downwards in the direction of being happy killers.

20 March 1991

John Pilger

I was against the use of armed force in liberating Kuwait. I was for using sanctions against Iraq, which would have been a more enlightened deployment of the UN in the cause of peace – and which, I believe, would have worked.

As for a lasting peace in the Middle East: this can only begin to happen when US and Israeli policy changes radically and the Palestinians are given a homeland, which is their fundamental human right.

3 April 1991

Ben Pimlott

Is it ever right to authorize the killing of 100,000 people, and indirectly cause the deaths of countless more, except in self-defence? The overwhelming majority of Britons, and a smaller proportion of Americans, Germans and Frenchmen (who had a more recent or a more devastating experience of the horrors of war) thought so, including some leftist bishops. Public and politicians alike were almost united in declaring it a just war. That was the most terrifying, 1914-evoking, thing about it.

The alternative to war was unpalatable and a bit humiliating: it usually is. Troops would have been needed to protect Saudi Arabia for a long time, sanctions alone would not have brought compliance with UN Resolutions, the coalition might have cracked. Meanwhile, Kuwait would have been brutalized and, quite possibly, repopulated. That is one set of possibilities: another included a chance that, after six months or a year of sanctions and diplomatic isolation, a face-saving formula could have been found involving withdrawal plus 'linkage' with the West Bank. Such an outcome would, indeed, have been a triumph for the New World `Order. Instead, Kuwait has been swiftly liberated, which is a matter for rejoicing. Against this achievement must be set the price. Thousands of teenage conscripts are dead, an ecological holocaust afflicts the Gulf, and a catastrophe has been visited on the Kurdish nation. There is also the destabilizing effect of the power vacuum caused by the collapse of Iraq in a tinderbox region. The cost of a temporary uplift to American military prestige will be a deepening of anti-Western revanchism through much of the Islamic world. Whether the demonstration that Crime Does Not Pay will inhibit stronger or less bankrupt countries than Iraq remains an open question.

What has the world learnt? That it was safer in the Cold War, when the American-Soviet mutual fear nipped incidents like this in the bud, and that the rewriting of Potsdam and Yalta which gives Moscow a free hand in the Baltic in return for a US free hand in the Middle East is fraught with danger. For psychopathic dictators and terrorists there is also the salutary lesson that modern wars are not to be fought with blunderbusses: we may expect the black market price of smart weapons to rise exponentially, until production can meet the new demand. It is only a matter of time now before the IRA, which used a crude home-made mortar against Downing Street, is equipped to turn Belfast or London into a Beirut. Finally there is a false message for armchair warriors and their leaders: that rich nations can once again win wars against poor nations at negligible cost to themselves. That was the true meaning of President Bush's exultant comment about the US kicking the Vietnam syndrome.

With a kill ratio of 500 to 1 (only 195 coalition troops died) this was a war without tears for the West: a clean, quick, telly war of tank-zapping entertainment, an exhilarating break from the recession. The troops were brave, the generals were efficient, the politicians kept their cool. It was one of the most obscene and portentous episodes of modern times.

26 March 1991

Peter Porter

I was against the use of force by the coalition of United Nations forces to liberate Kuwait. Not only did I distrust the motives of the Americans and their allies, I was sure that the devastation the war would cause would be an evil in its own right, and that no quantity of original evil in the form of Saddam Hussein's aggression could justify the horror which intervention would inevitably produce. This is precisely what has happened. That the Americans now hypocritically will not intervene further to stop the blood-letting as Saddam defends his regime goes to show that they can swap enemies as easily as principles. It appears to them to be a happier course to deal with villains than with Moslem fundamentalists.

I see no chance of lasting peace in the Middle East. Stability is our word for favourable arrangements politically and commercially.

27 March 1991

John Press

Reluctantly, I supported the use of armed force in the liberation of Kuwait. Despite the death of many civilians, the slaughter on the Basra Road and the wretched aftermath of the war I think that we were justified in fighting Saddam Hussein.

I have no idea about how to restore lasting peace and stability in the Middle East – indeed I doubt whether they have existed there since the days of the Pharaohs.

The Thirty Years War ended when various foreign powers no longer thought it profitable to foment the civil war in Germany; and when, despite the exhortations of religious fanatics, the inhabitants had become too exhausted to persist in their routine of massacre, rape and cannibalism. Perhaps, one day the unhappy peoples of the Middle East will reach a similar stage.

30 April 1991

James Purdy

I am opposed to almost all of the foreign policies undertaken by the United States for at least as long ago as Vietnam. The US invasion of Granada and Panama are violations of all international law. I do not approve of the US action to liberate Kuwait because it seems to me we have helped the government of Iraq for many years by giving Iraq arms to attack other Arab governments. Also the US sits idly by while Israel terrorizes and mistreats the Palestinians. Meanwhile the United States is falling to pieces at home. We have nearly 8,000,000 homeless, millions infected with AIDS, an almost total collapse of education for blacks, and a government which refuses to find other forms of energy outside of oil. Most Americans of voting age do not vote, so that the regimes of Reagan and Bush do not represent the American people who are in almost total eclipse. The press of the United States is not free, but a mouthpiece of powerful government and monopoly interests. The American people are brainwashed by a shoddy mendacious corrupt television, and by a corrupt multi-millionaire publishing empire. And look at what we have 'liberated' in Kuwait, a royal imperial tyranny which has starved and mistreated its powerless people.

16 March 1991

Frederic Raphael

These questions differ from those asked about Vietnam and the Falklands, since the outcome of the military action is now happily resolved. Happily? In my view, yes; imagine what consequences would have flowed from a stalemate or a disaster. That such an outcome was manifestly desired by those on the 'Left' who opposed resistance to Saddam Hussein is another instance of the deterioration of the 'socialist' ideology on which, to a greater or smaller degree, *bien-pensant* thought (including my own, to some degree) has been reliant for the last fifty years. As for the 'humanism' represented by CND (which could barely conceal the hope that the Americans would do something unforgivable), it too has lost its claim on our respect. Neither morally nor pragmatically can pacifism, in this case, be distinguished from cowardice or treachery.

It is plausible to find motives of self-advantage in the West's resistance to Hussein, but such motives are not incompatible with morality, nor necessarily undeserving of applause. The notion of 'liberation' is somewhat misleading: Kuwait was stolen and the theft has not been allowed to stand. One need not admire a man who has been robbed, nor does one sanction theft where the victim is less than admirable (or the thief intimidatingly well-armed). That laws are not universally enforced, or with the same zeal, is not an argument against their enforcement. The suggestion that Israel has 'stolen' land from those who sought her extinction in war, and lost, is merely another instance of spurious and almost certainly mischievous 'logic'.

The eviction of Iraq from Kuwait has been accompanied by despicable acts, all of them – so far as I know – by Saddam Hussein and his supporters. The ecological damage is appalling, but acquiescence in Iraq's appropriation would have been disastrous too. I would sooner rely on human ingenuity (and greed) to retrieve the mess than to have deferred to human depravity (and greed) and ignored it.

The second part of the question is, to a degree, as idle as it is disjunctive from the first. 'Lasting peace and stability' have scarcely been endemic in the region since Alexander's generals started to dispute the succession twenty-three hundred years ago. I have no more belief in any formula for their procurement than for one claiming to turn lead into gold. The ideological consensus is that the existence of Israel is to blame for the instability which, if retrospective accountancy is to be employed, the break-up of the Ottoman Empire by the Powers after 1918 largely procured. Israel's actions, like her existence and survival, please no universalizing Idea and hence are regularly condemned, not least by those who, alluding to the Jewish vote, find it improper that Jews should have any means, however marginal, to influence their destiny. The suggestion that 'the Arabs' (a single unit only according to parodic ideology) can be appeased by Israeli concessions, forced upon Jerusalem by the correctors of 'injustice', is mere moralizing, according to a table of morality which has no place in the canon of those who will supposedly be recruited to tranquillity by Israeli withdrawal. To speak of 'restoring' peace and stability is to imply that either colonialism or the Ottoman Empire might be reinstated, which is absurd. The chances of an improvement in stability depend on the dominant Powers ceasing to be inhibited by formulaic notions (and the guilt which follows them). The West is again in a position to lay down the law, and oversee its observation, and should be less apprehensive of 'public opinion' than of its own interests.

The relations between the West and the Arab states are fraught with falsities of all kinds; bogus respect and ranting demands have led to grotesque misreadings, of which Saddam's own estimate of himself was the last and greatest. I have no wish to see the Arabs belittled, but they must be brought – like all of us – to some rational sense of their own possibilities. I am glumly hopeful that piecemeal peace can be contrived between Israel and her neighbours, but not on the basis of 'trust' or of morality. The Syrians and the Israelis spend huge sums on mutual intimidation and cannot afford to do so; thus they do not need to trust each other in order to arrive at a mutually advantageous settlement. If, in due course, they can achieve constructive joint purposes, so much the better. There are, in fact, quite a few *de facto* agreements between Israel and her neighbours (the waters of the Jordan continue to flow freely), though no Arabs dare acknowledge them publicly. The respect paid to ignorant mobs and their 'feelings' simply sets a premium on the loudest malice. The time has come for interested parties to make local progress rather than to pursue some global 'justice' which, in practice, demands the destruction of Israel.

Any notion that the region can become nuclear-free, or that this would 'stabilize' it, is proposed only because it is known to its proposers that it will also entail – as if 'inadvertently' – the perpetual vulnerability and probable dismantling of Israel. It is advanced in order to disparage Israel rather than in order to secure her existence. There is, it is true, something 'unfair' in the prospect of Israel with nuclear weapons and her enemies without them, but it is an unfairness on which 'peace and stability' almost certainly depend. I should be glad to see a Palestinian state (to which Jordan, a wilfully created and factitious state, can well contribute territorially). Such a state will need to exchange the apocalyptic rhetoric of the PLO and its supporters, respectable and terroristic, for the mundane realities of practical management. Its 'dangers' for Israel will be very small and it will, with any luck, absorb the political energies of most – but never all – of those who today amalgamate in mischievous rant. No one has clearly said that the Arabs should be ashamed of themselves, not for failing to defeat Israel but for using their wealth so fatuously and for betraying the traditions which once made Arabic culture so extraordinary. The humbugging diplomacy of the West, flattering tyrants and *mafiosi*, has hampered political maturity. Western connivance with scoundrels winked at the repression of those who might, with the uses of civilized intelligence, have preferred education to religious dogma, and diplomacy to thuggery.

The only 'answer' to the second question is that Israel should be annihilated, as various 'dispassionate' arguments seem to require. This will not happen and hence there is no answer. I suspect that certain concessions (which I am sentimental enough to desire) can be 'forced' upon them, if only because they are really in the interests of a government which cannot make them voluntarily. Saddam Hussein's invasion of Kuwait had nothing to do with helping the Palestinian cause; the Palestinian cause was recruited to help Saddam Hussein. The Palestinians' opportunism was as 'understandable' as it was misguided, but since no state, Jewish or otherwise, can look forward to a perpetual social tension and violence, and since self-interest is the most persuasive of motives, it is to be hoped that Israel will find a way of retreating from repression. If the powers, like the Arabs, fear (rightly) that Israel will unleash thermo-nuclear war rather than acquiesce in her own liquidation, I am partial enough to think that that will be an excellent incentive for her enemies to accept what they need not applaud – her permanent place in the geography of the region. If magnanimity on Israel's part accompanies her intransigence, it will be a comfort to those of us who would prefer to think well of her. It would be as moving as it is improbable if the claims of the Kurds to self-determination – no less unreasonable than the Palestinians' – were to be honoured in the 'just settlement' which Arabists supposedly desire.

4 March 1991

Claire Rayner

I was very uneasy about accepting this invitation to line up behind one or other sets of flags in the dispute that keeps growling on in the Middle East. To take sides, even from (perhaps particularly from) the depths of a comfortable armchair well out of the line of fire is to collude in the hateful notion that warfare, with its emphasis on killing and destruction, is a logical and reasonable way to deal with human conflict.

I must here declare an interest. I am a devout and abiding hater of warfare. I can't help being, as I have been labelled by some, lily-livered. It's an attitude that was ingrained in me in earliest childhood; in 1940, at the age of nine, I spent twenty-eight hours under seven feet of Blitz-created rubble in the East End of London, waiting for someone to come and fetch me out. An experience of this nature does concentrate the mind somewhat, and it had the effect of concentrating mine into the notion that fighting is stupid, that dropping bombs that bury people in broken houses is stupid and that any person who believes war is inevitable is stupid.

I am not sufficiently naïve to believe that conflict is avoidable. As long as one man has two pieces of bread and another none there will be anger and greed and desire to do harm to that other person (the two-piece man hating the no-piece man as fervently, of course, as the no-piecer loathes the two-piecer). I know there will be arguments, attempts to beguile, to rob, to equivocate – but there does not have to be a descent into physical attack. We have tongues in our heads, and brains in our skulls; surely we can resolve our bread and all other arguments with these tools rather than with sticks and stones that all too rapidly grow into nuclear, chemical and biological bombs?

This then is my basic belief; and to see two armies at violent odds with each other in the Gulf from January of this year, after several months of feinting and growling and posing and generally making bellicose noises at each other, made me sick.

Literally. Like many other people sitting filled with a sense of helplessness on the side lines, I suffered in those months a collection of symptoms of physical disorder that reflected the distress going on in my mind as news bulletins spread like rancid oil on a marble slab to invade every corner of the day. I watched soldiers resurrecting World War Two gestures of thumbs up solidarity and loving it. I watched flag-waggers weeping luxuriously as they Waved Our Brave Lads Goodbye and watched and listened in fury as cheap newspapers whipped up all the hatred they could against Them, the Enemy. The five-legged fire-breathing ten-eyed baby-eating Iraqis – or whatever it is they were trying to make the more simple-minded amongst us believe. I watched American and British pilots and generals chortling as they played their bar-room computer games – pow, wham, killed you, you bastard, let's kick ass — with real weapons on real human beings. I listened as serious, thoughtful, concerned commentators – ostensibly educated people – played their sandbox games as they pushed model tanks and missiles around to explain to the rest of the world just what was going on in those far away battlefields. And I remembered Tom Paine saying, in his preface to *The Rights of Man* 'That there are men in all countries who get their living by war, and by keeping the quarrels of nations, is as shocking as it is true'.

Those horrible people, every one of them who was there in the war by choice (I can't speak of conscripts on the Iraqi side, of course) and all the busy 'analysts' were having a lovely time and in many cases getting cash for doing so. Soldiers itching 'to get going' as they squatted in the desert waiting to be told to start the killing; generals at last justifying their existences as they planned the wholesale destruction of as man y people as possible; (combatants for choice but they'd settle happily enough for civilians if that was all they could get in their sights – vide the bombing of the Baghdad 'bunker'), old generals and assorted army detritus beaming away in the television studio lights and being deferred to by journalists (who should have known better) as though their 'analyses' were actually worth something – the whole thing was and still is revolting.

This whole war, I am convinced, had one function only and still has (because it's not over yet, is it?) It's all to do with the aggrandisement and enrichment of arms manufacturers and the users of oil. No one gave a damn about the sins of Saddam Hussein when he destroyed vast numbers of Kurdish people and treated others of the citizenry of his own country as totally expendable (using Western-provided arms to do it with, of course) and they still don't. He can start doing it all over again as long as he obeys warfare rules that have been made by his erstwhile enemies.

I hold no brief for Saddam Hussein and his aspirations. The man is clearly not fit to be running a country and has been allowed to grab far too much power. But I cannot be convinced that the only way to depose him is kill hundreds of thousands of his compatriots. Dammit, that was done and he's *still* there and still doing heaven knows what to the people under his thumb he doesn't like.

He could have been chilled out of power. The various sanctions against trade that those who oppose his regime could apply would have worked had they been applied with real enthusiasm and given time to have their effect. Yes, of course Iraqis other than Saddam Hussein would have suffered, experienced shortages and so forth, just as ordinary black South Africans did when the same technique was applied against the white oppressors there; but would the Iraqis have been any worse off than they are now, living in their country after it has been hammered to a pulp by war?

So, to answer the first question I was asked to address in this discussion, and although the warfaring phase of the Gulf Conflict seems to be at present over with a cease-fire currently in force, I have to say I was against the use of armed force in 'liberating' Kuwait (much good liberation has done that pathetic piece of sand! Burning oil wells, ruined electricity, water, sewers, hospital, food distribution and other essential services – it's great to be Free!) and I still am.

What about the second question asked – how can lasting peace and stability be restored to the Middle East?

That's a specious question; it implies there has at some golden past time been a prolonged period of stability and peace in the Middle East. I've checked through the history books carefully and I find no record of such a time. It has ever since Biblical days been a simmering hotbed of tribal wars, and their successors, national wars. The arrival on the scene in 1948 of Israel, planted arbitrarily in the middle of an already unstable area by Westerners with their own rows to hoe ensured that there would be continuous strife in this cradle of civilization. (When I stop and think that here in Babylon, in old Canaan, in Mesopotamia in general, human thought at its most valuable budded, blossomed and came to fruit in alphabets, in mathematical systems, in science and philosophy and literature, it breaks my heart. Can't we have this sort of intellectual ferment without the other sort, greed and anger and demands for ever more territory?)

If I were asked how we might attempt to bring peace and stability for the first time in the Middle East I'd suggest three steps.

A more urgent search for alternative energy sources to oil, the existence of which in that arid soil has led to much of the upheaval we've known recently and even more to cruel inequalities in social structures.

An equally urgent search for reasonably priced irrigation and soil renewal techniques that would make said arid soils fertile enough to offer different sources of wealth and security to all the area's inhabitants.

And of course an intelligently planned and sensibly run conference, the outcome of which would definitely be applied, about what needs to be done to accommodate both Israel's hunger for space and the Palestinian demands for a home of *their* own.

Will any of these, especially the last, lead to peace and stability? I can't possibly say. I think they could help. But I can say this much; they'd be a damned sight more practical and human and useful than what's been going on in the Middle East in this first trimester of 1991. Hundreds of thousands of Iraqis killed (while Westerners crow 'Hardly any casualties, hooray, hooray') has been a disgusting blot on human history. *Another* disgusting blot. When, oh when will we *learn*?

26 March 1991

John Rety

Although I was there on the night of 15 January with the protesters against the war in Parliament Square, in a group of friends and I sang with all my heart the undulating words of 'All we are saying is give peace a chance', today, five months later, a piece of my life has vanished. Like a cornered would-be victim who somehow escapes; after the heart-pangs, the fear, the desperate knowledge that death is round the corner, ensued by the questions of why me, why now, why in these particular circumstances, without reason, without dignity, and with the realization that life has no meaning, no justice, no language and the other realization that as suddenly as the atrocity begins, it has suddenly ended.

A hand clasping my hand had more meaning on that night than all of human knowledge packed in to a wise man's satchel. The comparison is edifying. Human shouts, laughter, tears, desperation, compassion and that terrible hush in that historic square on the stroke of midnight when those big bells acknowledged our presence. No, not all were there for peace, some for love and some for lust. The dark night hides its secrets.

But today, the questions addressed to the writer, not the quasi-human being, produces a different kind of dismay. For to quote a line from an earlier poem, 'Song of Anarchy', 'That is just thinking after the event'. We are pretty good at that. But is it enough?

I have difficulty in answering [your first] question in brief, for I do not regard it as a first premise. Once such a question can be asked an agreement on all that has gone before has to be assumed and there is no such agreement. Nevertheless, I am against war, which I regard as a superimposition on communal life. From this it may follow that war being a superimposition on communal life, I am also against the idea of armed forces which superimpose war on communal life. Therefore I cannot accept that the superimposing armed forces can by definition 'liberate' the contents of a matchbox, never mind the geographical phantasy masquerading under the name of Kuwait.

But even if the political boundaries and demarcation lines have been chalked up by men in yellow plastic overalls, what I did protest against and shall never cease to protest against is the people (poor animals) being bombed out of existence, and of having let loose the worst combination of human endeavour: Religion, Repression and Regimentation.

We can have peace only if we understand what peace is, or what we mean by peace. Our best writers and philosophers have wearied themselves through the centuries in spelling out what the human family should aim for. No doubt we can have peace, once we know what peace is and if we want peace. If by peace we mean that nobody should rebel against tyranny, against despotism, that whoever the ruler is, is better than the ruler who will follow, then we are clearly advocating stability, by no means the same thing as peace. We cannot define peace as long as there are prisons, as long as there is inequality of wealth, of opportunity, where those with the sharpest tongue and weapons rule over the meek and mild. Such people despise fairy tales. Once upon a time there was a land of milk and honey, how laughable. But there is no other truth than the truth of the imagination. War is no proof that peace is impossible; it is merely that human beings are coerced to co-operate for the sake of futility. What we have proved through the Gulf War is that we are still mechanical creatures who have learnt to co-ordinate our actions. There we are in the sky, dropping bombs. There we are below, sheltering and huddling. The roles are interchangeable, the acting is superb, but the writing is not as good as Ovid's. Perhaps he is still worth quoting: 'In the beginning was the Golden Age, when people of their own accord, without threat of punishment, without laws, maintained good faith and did what was right'. We have been in the iron age long enough.

1 June 1991

Alan Ross

Initially against so one-sided a use of force, once action was taken I supported it. I would have preferred only a United Nations flag to have been carried and the fact that all military operations were under the auspices of the United Nations to have been emphasized.

The nervous and abrupt termination of hostilities, though understandable, nevertheless left thousands of Kurds and Shias in the lurch, their originally encouraged rebellions condemned to peter out with predictable consequences, and the *status quo* in Iraq unchallenged. This cannot surely have been what those taking part had in mind. It appears to have been nothing more complicated than a loss of nerve.

It remains to be seen whether, in the next six months, the refugee problem can be contained. If it can, and the Israelis, Palestinians and other interested parties show a greater willingness for compromise than hitherto, then just conceivably an international conference could come up with acceptable ideas. But one wouldn't like to bet on it.

7 May 1991

Carol Rumens

Kuwait was invaded by a power-obsessed dictator and it was 'liberated' by a man equally power-crazed but, since he is not a dictator and his power is decided by a process at least partly democratic, desperate for electoral credibility. The *liberation of Kuwait* is a euphemism for the valorisation of Bush. Of course, oil may have had a little to do with it too. 'Oil' is the Middle East's wealth and its tragedy. When someone has something the others hungrily covet, it brings out the worst sort of behaviour in those others.

The Middle East both punishes itself by the horrific, mighty grip of that phoniest male leader of all, God, and suffers the aftermath of Western empire-building over the last two centuries – French, British, American. The best thing we could do for the area is back off and stop all interference other than humanitarian aid. And, of course, work together to devise a new, internationalist ten commandments of good behaviour. Until some kind of ethical code of values is brought back to politics we will lurch from horror to horror. The arms-trade for example, must be outlawed. Disarmament can no longer be a matter of getting rid of nuclear weapons but of winding down the whole war-machine to something minimally instead of maximally destructive. We need to form international think-tanks with a real power of veto in the case of deciding whether or not to go to war. We must empower the psychologists and philosophers and ecologists, and create a new kind of leader – one who is a linguist, a listener and above all a secularist. At the height of the crisis I heard Saddam, Bush and Major, all, within minutes of each other, calling on their particular version of God for help. That memory is in a way the most depressing of them all. There is no shortage of terrible memories: the great mangled scrap-heap of the road to Basra, the Iraqi woman who screamed at us to look into her eyes and remember, the soldier melted to a Frankenstein's monster in his tank . . . many more. But what is as coldly chilling to the spine as the sound of three grown men, three national leaders, calling on God to help them with their war? That alone makes me despair for the human race.

* * * * *

When we were waiting to hear the outcome of the Soviet peace proposals, we sat in the kitchen listening to the TV and the Russian stations on short-wave radio, just in case the wonderful thing should happen. I didn't expect it, and I knew Gorbachev's motives were no less self-interested than anyone else's, but at least his was a *peace*-plan, not a plan for massive blood-shed. So I was holding my breath despite my attempts at cynicism, and then feeling increasing despair as Bush embarked on his bluster. It may well have been that Saddam would not have honoured any agreement to withdraw, but he should have been given that option. The Russians, I think, understand more about the Arab art of bargaining so that neither side loses face: their psychology was all along more subtle than that of the other negotiators, and their will to succeed, for whatever reasons, was genuine.

Everything seemed heightened on the day of the deadline: I do not remember ever having been stirred to such a state of emotional tension by a public event. An image kept coming into my head – something Yura told me about his father who had been a high-ranking officer in the Russian Navy but, in his retirement, had taken to the gentler arts of gardening and cookery. He had acquired a real Samurai sword from Japan, and now regularly used it, because of its fine edge, for chopping cabbage. This image suddenly seemed full of significance. Perhaps the idea of using a sledge-hammer to crack a nut is contained in its somewhere, but more important I think is that it symbolizes the idea of handling something very dangerous with great artistry and care until finally good comes of it – beating a sword into a ploughshare is a dangerous act, psychologically at least! If you want to go further you can say it represents the replacement of aggressive masculinity by the feminine principle, something which happens to most normal men (excluding, of course, power-crazed national leaders) as they grow older, and which I used to think would finally happen globally. I don't think so now. I think the masculine principle will devastate the world long before it has mellowed into wisdom. You don't need an atom bomb — a match will do it.

3 April 1991

Pierre Salinger

If the US and other Western powers had understood what Saddam Hussein was saying, his invasion of Kuwait would have been prevented and the war avoided.

6 May 1991

Vernon Scannell

Whether or not the Gulf War was bound to happen I firmly believe that peaceful negotiations were never given a fair chance of success and that the

United States, aided and abetted by Britain, were from the start intent upon a full-scale military show-down, the virtually certain success of which would go some way towards wiping out the humiliation of their defeat and disgrace in Vietnam. The savage allied bombing of civilians in Kuwait and Iraq almost certainly exacerbated the scale of the vengeful atrocities committed by the Iraqis before their retreat from Kuwait.

In Britain Her Majesty's Opposition, with a few honourable exceptions, feebly fell in behind the Tory patriotic parade just as they did in the Falklands episode for which, incidentally, we are still paying heavily. The triple-echo effect of the Bush, Major, Kinnock martial utterances would have been comic in a fictional context but were sickening when one knew that thousands of human lives were at stake. I know that something had to be done about Saddam's annexation of Kuwait but the questions of what and by whom were never properly addressed.

I see no more hope for peace and stability in the Middle East after the Gulf War than there was before it: if anything the possibility will be even more remote.

1 March 1991

Peter Scupham

I was in favour of using armed force, but considered that this was to effect the dismantling of a cancerous, unfocused military machine, with Kuwait's liberation a lucky pretext, at a time when economic, military, and 'moral' options could be synchronized without the risks of a super-power confrontation. *Realpolitik* made such an intervention internationally tolerable; the military mis-match made the campaign's brilliance sickeningly depressing. It was a surprise to find the Hidden Agenda, Saddam's overthrow, was not on the Hidden Agenda list.

For lasting peace and stability, go to the Holy Mountains of the psyche where lions and lambs graze together – they can no more be secured in the Middle East than anywhere else in the world, though that doesn't invalidate our fallible attempts to make our crooked hearts love their crooked neighbours.

12 May 1991

Brocard Sewell

I do not think that returning Kuwait to the exploitative oil-rich dynasty that previously controlled it can properly be described as 'liberation'; but in any case I am opposed to all war on principle.

In my opinion the key to lasting peace and stability in the Middle East lies in the surrender by Israel of all 'Occupied Territories', and the creation of Jerusalem as an internationalized religious city outside the State of Israel.

20 May 1991

Alan Sillitoe

War is dreadful for soldiers and civilians alike, and no one who has heard the whistle of a descending bomb can think otherwise. In case anyone does, photographs of carnage from the battlefield are there to convince.

Yet in the twentieth century war seems to have become —more so than at other times – a condition of human existence, and may well continue to be so into the twenty-first century as well. The fact that war breaks out, or is courted, or is responded to – often a little too readily, and certainly too often – is always a disaster. Occasionally, however, a war has to take place in order to avoid a future conflict which reason says would be very much worse.

Being for the war, I consider it a mistake that the Allied armies did not go all the way to Baghdad and depose Saddam Hussein – though perhaps there was no need, since few such leaders survive the rout of their army. The common assumption that one must not humiliate a country in defeat is a puerile argument. It could be said that Germany and Japan were humiliated at the end of the Second World War, and now, forty-six years later, neither nation contributed one soldier to the effort against Iraq.

In five or so years Saddam Hussein's rockets would have had the range to reach not only Israel but southern Europe. If the Allies had not made war on Iraq Israel would sooner or later have been forced to fight on her own. Thus it is the first conflict in the Middle East which for many reasons has been fought by other nations to Israel's advantage.

It is a common fallacy also that Israel has always been a disturbing factor in the Middle East. If Israel had not existed a man like Saddam Hussein would have been forced to invent it. The Gulf War has not been fought for Israel, however, yet Israel deserves to become a beneficiary due to not having responded when attacked with Scud missiles, and also because of its presence in the area.

Saddam Hussein would have sooner or later attacked Israel even if the so-called Palestinian problem had been resolved. The Arabs in general have long been encouraged to assume, and to go on hoping, that the solution to the 'Palestinian Problem' will only be complete when all of Israel has been taken over by them. A PLO country based on Judea, Samaria and Gaza would be seen as one stage in this process.

Jordan should become a country for the Palestinians. Nations are formed out of adversity. Jordan is but the other part of old Mandated Palestine, and Israel the western half between the River Jordan and the Mediterranean Sea. Such a solution would stabilize the area and make it prosperous.

Iraq would slowly recover and even increase its standard of living if Saddam Hussein went, and the money gained from oil was not spent on armaments. Such a peace would make the area safe for a long time to come.

4 March 1991

An infusion of Machiavelli's pragmatism might have helped to leave Iraq more peaceful than it is. 'When you strike at a prince, kill him. Do not leave him wounded, howsoever wounded he may be, unless mortally so.' If the Allies in the Gulf War had continued the offensive even for another forty-eight hours the wily Saddam Hussein (who will live to fight another day) would not have had enough of an army left to harry the Kurds.

Nationalism has been the bane of the twentieth century, for most of which time it has been encouraged by various Powers in their backing of any ethnic group to further their own ends. As a concept it has been generally disastrous, especially for the ethnic groups themselves.

The Kurds have brought much of the present distress on themselves, yet it has also been forced upon them. Saddam Hussein's defeat would have encouraged them to renew their rebellion in any case, with advice from no one. It is one of the many crises in their history, which they will survive as they have survived others. The only hope is that they will eventually be able to live at peace with their host countries, including Iraq.

An independent Kurdistan would certainly destabilize not only Iraq but Persia and Turkey as well, creating another conflict which would once again devastate much of the Middle East.

In supplying the Kurds with humanitarian aid, the United States of America and other countries are doing what they can to ameliorate the sufferings of women and children. Yet one is perfectly aware that it is the Kurdish 'fighters' who will have first choice of all supplies dropped or sent in. This will be to make sure their 'army' remains intact so as to resume fighting for an independent state in the future. Such nationalistic intentions will make it even more unlikely that Iraq (preferably under a humane government and a different leader) will recover from its recent tragedy.

25 April 1991

Robert Skidelsky

The end of the Cold War offered a chance to apply the doctrine of collective security for the first time since 1945, and I am glad it was taken to expel Saddam Hussein from Kuwait. The principle that states have no right simply to seize their neighbours, accepted by everyone, had to be upheld. That much seems clear to me.

However, the principle of collective security needs to be reinforced by a strengthened machinery for the peaceful settlement of disputes. Oil wealth, owing to the accidents of history and geography, is unduly concentrated on a rather small number of people, and should, no doubt, be more equitably distributed. If it is not, it will be a standing source of grievance and instability in the region.

Although the damage Iraq did to Kuwait is immense, we should not try to extract anything more than very moderate reparations from Iraq. The Iraqis have to rebuild their country too. As the aftermath of the first world war showed, the attempt to extract large reparations from a defeated enemy can easily sow the seeds of a new conflict.

22 March 1991

Colin Spencer

I have a profound loathing of war and the military machine, childhood memories of Hitler and Belsen atrocities have remained screamingly vivid. Hence, I was all for sanctions continuing against Iraq, but regrettably I have had to admit that war is a necessary evil against psychotic dictators. I think Saddam Hussein should be tried for crimes against humanity. It is urgently necessary that the United Nations (who have gained moral strength throughout the Gulf War) become an ethical world conscience and use its considerable powers to intervene against all gross inhumanities. But they refused to in the past over Pol Pot, Chile and Uganda. They should begin now.

It is a great and tragic irony that the world religions divide peoples into opposing camps of such vehement bitterness, when at their core they spread the same message of compassion for your brother, whatever his race or creed. Why should not religious leaders be responsible for their flock and be held to be so in international law? There is a historical precedent for such a view. (Arrest the Pope and the Archbishop of Canterbury for the war in Ulster, I say). Yet to teach that central message of brotherly love, instead of inflaming their flock with indignant loathing for the supposed enemy, could do much to lessen tension. Muslims, Hindus, Jews and Christians of all denominations should have a solid education in a book like Huxley's *The Perennial Philosophy*, then perhaps we might be closer to peace in the world.

16 April 1991

John Sweeney

The video game to end all video games left me feeling queasy. This did not look like a war; wasn't one, until my paper [*The Observer*] printed the picture of the charred skull of the unknown Iraqi soldier. The skull was a necessary corrective to the bleached-out blandness of the war. Still, it was hard to think of any other way of pushing Saddam Hussein back. So, yes, I was for the use of armed force in liberating Kuwait.

And peace in the Middle East? That requires the death of Saddam Hussein, a fair deal for the Kurds, security for the Israelis and, of course, a homeland for the Palestinians. But – as Saddam's gunships zap the Kurds – despair seems the only realistic emotion. Despair and disgust that, having set up the war machine, the West stood by and staged tinkling victory parades while Saddam continued to kill.

5 April 1991

D.M. Thomas

Before the Gulf War started, I was – like the British public in general – eighty-five per cent. in favour of launching it.

One of the most evil and aggressive dictators in the world had taken over a helpless, peaceable country and was terrorizing its people. I strongly doubted if sanctions would work; and if we made concessions – say giving them a few oil wells, as Mr Heath was advocating – Saddam's triumph would be immense and he'd be all set to become a nuclear superpower in the region.

The small part of me that hesitated did so because of the devastation, death and suffering that war would cause; because one could not be absolutely certain sanctions would fail, if given longer; and because I knew I'd be bitterly angry if any son of mine were to be killed in such a distant war.

Also I had to recognize an atavistic urge in me to see some action, to see this monster destroyed, as dramatically and completely as possible. I felt guilty about my own aggression – which I would expect others to carry through and perhaps die for. I therefore respected the pacifists, but not the appeasers.

When the war began, I supported the effort wholeheartedly, and I still do. I think it's become clear that sanctions would not have worked in time, if at all. Either the coalition would have started crumbling, or Kuwait would have ceased to exist, or both. Dictators don't worry if their people starve. The war was tragic, but had to be, to prevent worse evil. I think my feelings were in line with those of the British people at large. Probably, in this, I differed from most writers and artists, as I had done over the Falklands War. I did not feel unhappy to be more in tune with popular feeling than with 'intellectuals'. I didn't envy them their gift for finding complications and moral dilemmas everywhere, nor their immunity to vulgar emotions like patriotism.

The much-maligned tabloids, which often presented brilliantly vivid reports, were closer to reality than the cogent arguments of such commentators as Bradford University's Lecturer in 'peace studies', Paul Rogers, who predicted the land war would last for many months. I assume he has taken voluntary redundancy.

I am delighted that several over-inflated balloons were pricked by the stunning victory. The arrogant egotism of Mr Heath and Mr Healey have been punctured; though, like Saddam's newscasters, I don't suppose they will notice. The *Guardian*'s ragged Saddamite army of teachers, social workers, media persons and women's groups have also been scattered. It is worth recalling that the *Guardian* leader, when Saddam invaded Kuwait, accepted that the occupation was irreversible. Fortunately Mrs Thatcher and President Bush felt otherwise. The *Guardian*, Mr Heath and Mr Healey are all notably pro-European; and one of their motives for counselling eternal negotiation may have been their knowledge that the conflict would burst the bubble of European union. The war has demonstrated that the special relationship, founded in the deep emotional ties of wartime alliance, is still strong; whereas the European idea is an abstraction. I hope and believe the concept of our pooling sovereignty with a navel-gazing Germany and its minions has received a fatal wound.

Many writers will say it was all for oil. It was of course partly for oil; but I don't think one should back away from doing what is right simply because it is also in one's interest to do so. Likewise our having helped to build up Saddam should not prevent us from trying to rectify our past errors: quite the contrary. This has been a victory for justice and freedom. President Bush, Mr Major, Mrs Thatcher, and the coalition's generals and servicemen, deserve our gratitude. We can be proud of our country's part in the conflict, and a justifiable pride breeds a healthy optimism. Believing that the USA is generally a force for good, I am pleased about its re-won confidence also.

For the future, the arms traffickers, traders in death, must be stopped. The West and the United Nations must now show an equal determination to achieve justice for the Palestinians; the ex-terrorists in the Knesset must be brought to heel, just as Saddam has been. And the Gulf States, including Kuwait, must be encouraged towards democracy. As the Foreign Secretary observed during this crisis, no two democratic countries have ever gone to war with each other.

4 March 1991

Sue Townsend

I hated everything about the Gulf War – the jingoism, the nationalism and the cowardly gits who sent young men to die for oil. Because the pub bores were right – oil and money and American Emperialism were at the heart of this war.

I knew when I was being fed propaganda and I was horrified to discover that other people – too many — swallowed everything they were told. Like children, I was lonely – outside my own family very few people spoke out and said that the war was a farce – a hypocritical farce. To my shame I did not join any demonstrations against the war. But I wanted to.

The aftermath has proved to be disastrous in every way. The reviled Dictator is still dictating, the Kuwaitis are persecuting the Palestinians, there is massive ecological damage and Iraq is devastated and its people are suffering. The last few days of the war, when the allies bombed the retreating and cowed Iraqi troops, is a shameful and disgraceful episode.

I'm sorry but I blame the male impulse for bloodlust. It is ever present, just below the surface. We are far from being civilized. I include myself in this condemnation, because I did not speak out at the time. Afraid of being just another leftie.

1 July 1991

Geoffrey Trease

My own confident youthful pacifism shrivelled in the 1930s, when I saw how Gandhi would have fared against a Nazi gauleiter rather than a British viceroy. So I favoured our recent armed action in the Gulf and am only sorry that it took so long to launch. I see that under the existing circumstances this was unavoidable. Coalition casualties might have been as frightful as prophesied if action had been premature, so, deplorably, hapless Kuwaitis had to suffer some months longer. But I can see no alternative except a permanent – and adequate – United Nations force, not only for 'peace-keeping' but if need be peace-restoring and punitive, ready to turn out as urgently as a fire brigade. All the diplomatic discussion should be done beforehand, on clearly defined general principles, not while the house is burning down. A large-scale frontier-violation is obvious enough. Has not Nato indicated that such collective preparations are feasible?

I can see no other hope for 'restoring lasting peace and stability in the Middle East'. Restoring? When was there any since the Turkish Empire (rotten though it was) fragmented into sovereign states? Will the Arab states agree on *anything*, much less accept the existence of Israel? Will the Israelis become less intransigent? However daunting the task, the United Nations must create, if not a policeman on the beat, a riot-car of overwhelming superiority which can be rushed quickly to the scene of the affray.

6 May 1991

Edward Upward

I think the Gulf War (1) was a neo-imperialist war fought to ensure the continuing domination of the Middle East by the major Western powers, primarily America. (2) Its massive destruction of human life was intended as a warning of what would happen if any other local tyrant like Saddam Hussein acted against the interests of the neo-imperialists who had hitherto encouraged him. (3) It could be a very profitable war for them, from contracts to re-build what they have destroyed, and it might help America and Britain to recover from their current 'recession' – or it might not, and they might find themselves in for the worst slump yet. (4) Millions of men, women and children will go hungry, and even more will die of starvation, because of this war and because of the continuing exploitation of the poorer by the richer nations. (5) This war may mark a turning point after which the exploited peoples of the world, in the homelands of imperialism as well as in the impoverished countries, will begin to understand that united action by them against the imperialists is more important than national loyalty. I see little sign of this yet, but there seems no other way of preventing the polluting competitiveness of the imperialists from destroying the human race.

11 March 1991

Auberon Waugh

I was, and remain, against the use of armed force in 'liberating' Kuwait. I do not think it is any of my business to restore lasting peace and stability to the Middle East and therefore have no opinion on the matter. I wish I could be more helpful.

5 May 1991

Arnold Wesker

Saddam Hussein is a street-corner urchin who grew up to become a dangerously murderous fool.

There was never any doubt in my mind that armed force should oust his armies from Kuwait. More, because I believe the citizens of a country should be free to choose the leaders they want I hoped legitimate reasons would be found to enable the allied forces to move into Iraq and ensure the overthrow of Saddam together with his bully boys and the establishment of a democratic constitution giving the Iraqi people a legal framework of freedom to choose. I even fantasized about Iraq becoming a model state from which sanity and democracy would spread throughout the region.

There are depressing voices of cant in the air which declare it is not the business of the West to interfere and impose its doctrines upon a poor Arab nation. The Iraqis are not poor, they had – still have – riches beneath their feet to make them one of the most sophisticated and enlightened countries in the Middle East. It is often those same voices which insist, correctly, upon the responsibility of the West to give aid to disease and famine-struck regions. At the social and political level, not the private, we are all each others' business, not only because of moral considerations but simply because it can't be helped, it's such an inter-related, inter-dependent world.

But questions have to be answered. Where was the world when Russia invaded Afghanistan or when Argentina invaded the Falklands or when Israel invaded Lebanon? (And I ask this last as a very fierce defender of Israel's right to an independent existence). The legitimate government of Kuwait has to be defended, but is any government legitimate that is not democratically elected? Where were the spy satellites when Iraq prepared to invade? Did the Americans know of the invasion before it took place? Why did the US, France and Russia sell weapons, including chemical ones, to a known unstable political leader? Is it true that the CIA helped put or keep Hussein in power hoping he could be relied upon to stand up against Iran? When outbreaks of war here and there can endanger the lives and industry of so many hard-working and innocent people, when whole economies can be shaken by issues which have nothing to do with them, should arms continue to be, in the name of private enterprise, a product for sale on the free market? Since oil touches every aspect of everyone's life in the entire world shouldn't it be subject to an international agreement ensuring its free flow despite any eventuality?

I don't hold up much hope for peace in the area until the sweet Arab nature stops falling in love with the sound of itself being windily ardent instead of thoughtful, and until Islam surrenders its role as the state. If we are talking about the injustice of imposition then the existence of God with his incomprehensible ways must be the private belief of the individual not a belief imposed by bigoted priests. Religious tolerance, and freedom of the individual to believe what he or she wants, are among the most precious doctrines the West has to offer.

Of course the national sovereignty of other states forbids any one state imposing such doctrines but I've never understood how the prescription of freedom can be deemed an imposition. Martin Woollacott, more an authority on the area than I am, wrote succinctly, in *The Guardian*, 4 March, that in any discussion of the Arab predicament the issue of freedom in the Arab world and 'the question of rationality must obtrude . . . What is lacking in political and economic life is also often lacking in educational and intellectual life as well. How else to explain the extraordinary failure of rational thought that so often marks the Arabs at times of crisis?'

Nor do I think there will be peace until the Arabs cleanse themselves of their fratricidal hatred of Jews which has poisoned them, as it has poisoned many others, over the centuries.

8 March 1991

Colin Wilson

Like everybody else, I tended to be pro-Saddam when he started a war with Iran, simply because, like everybody else in the west, I found the Ayatollah pretty detestable. Like most other sensible people, I hate religious fanaticism, and it seemed to me that if the Ba'ath party is more or less secular, then I greatly preferred it to the Ayatollah's hell-fire brand of Islam.

And I must admit that, like most people in the west, I didn't even get too indignant when I learned about his gassing of Kurds – I was inclined to think that, on closer investigation, it would probably turn out to be another one of those atrocity stories without real foundation.

Light dawned on me quite suddenly after the shooting of that journalist Farzad Bazoft. Oddly enough, I had an intuition in the middle of the night that he was going to be shot, and heard it on the news the next morning. And the reason I had the intuition was that the news about the arrest of Bazoft somehow convinced me that Saddam Hussein belongs to the type that Van Vogt described as the 'Right Man' or the 'Violent Man' – a man who under no circumstances whatever, will ever admit that he is in the wrong. He lives in a kind of fantasy world in which he is a kind of Haroun al Rashid, and would ideally like to be a God who can throw thunderbolts. You will find a long chapter about the 'Right Man' in my book *A Criminal History of Mankind*, where I point out that they are absolute bastards to their wives and families, because of this peculiar fantasy that they are absolute despots who must under any circumstances be contradicted. If you actually prove a Right Man to be in the wrong, he will hit you in the face rather than admit it. (Oddly enough, if his wife leaves him, the Right Man very often goes completely to pieces or even commits suicide – she has pulled away the foundation of his tower of self-delusion.)

And when that little cunt Gerald Kaufman jumped up in parliament and said that if Saddam Hussein dared to do anything to Bazoft it would be the worst for him, I knew suddenly that nothing would be more likely than to make Saddam meet the challenge by instantly executing the journalist.

After that, I realized that he was an incredibly dangerous man, and that somehow he had to be stopped. So while many of my pacifist friends told me that it would be an act of sheer wickedness to start a war at this time in history, I never had the least doubt that somehow Saddam had to go – just like Hitler, or Idi Amin, or General Noriega. When we were in San Francisco, we saw some march of pacifists protesting that all the Americans really cared about was the oil in Kuwait. I honestly feel that this is not true. I think that all decent people were absolutely horrified when he marched into Kuwait

– although I was extremely interested to discover subsequently that apparently he did so because the Kuwaitis flatly refused to give way to his demands, and more or less dared him to invade Kuwait. It is always extremely dangerous to dare a Right Man to do anything – he will always do it, even if he knows it is going to cost him his life. You could put a pistol to a Right Man's head and dare him to hit you in the face, and he would still do it.

So although I knew perfectly well that he would carry out his threat of setting the oil wells on fire and turning Kuwait into 'a sea of blood', I never had the slightest doubt at any point that he had to be challenged. There is no point whatever in appeasing that kind of person. Fortunately, his type is not as numerous as one might suppose. But the one thing that is absolutely certain is that when a man like Saddam Hussein appears, it is extremely important for the world to oppose him, in spite of all his talk about seas of blood and revenge. (I see that he has announced Bush and John Major will remain targets for assassination for the rest of their lives.) On this point, I am completely in agreement with Bush – that what the United Nations have done is to demonstrate that at this point in the twentieth century, dictators can no longer get away with it. They've been doing it for the past 3,000 years or so – and I think it important to make sure that Saddam Hussein is one of the last.

7 March 1991

Sloan Wilson

An event as big as liberating Kuwait is bound to have both good and bad results. In the future it may discourage a few small-time aggressors and it has caused a jolly splurge of patriotism and confidence in the US which was badly needed after Vietnam. On the other hand, I hate saving Emirs and I much doubt that we have created anything like lasting peace in the Middle East. I mourn the tens of thousands of people of whatever country or religion who were killed there. I wish President Bush had used the billions we spent on this military extravaganza for reducing our dependence on oil and developing new sources of energy, My main feeling about the Middle East is that we should have nothing to do with it. This old Yankee says, 'Yankee go home and stay there!'

20 March 1991

Denis Winter

The military-industrial complexes of Western Europe and the USA first built Saddam up, then tested their own murderous toyshop of weaponry on his people. Military intelligence meanwhile, so effectively deployed against many thinking people at home, proved unable to predict the use Saddam Hussein would make of his own weaponry until a few days before the invasion.

When will governments have the courage to take a scalpel to this parasite?

And when will governments release more than a tithe of the information required for laymen to be able to make a significant contribution on key issues like the stability of the Middle East?

12 March 1991